Jan. 2016

THE CONSCIOUS PARENT'S GUIDE TO

Autism

A mindful approach for helping your child focus and succeed

Marci Lebowitz, OT

WITHDRAWN

Avon, Massachusetts

Published by

Adams Media, a division of F+W Media, Inc.

57 Littlefield Street, Avon, MA 02322. U.S.A.

www.adamsmedia.com

Contains material adapted from *The Everything® Parent's Guide to Children with Autism, 2nd Edition* by Adelle Jameson Tilton, copyright © 2010, 2004 by F+W Media, Inc., ISBN 10: 1-4405-0392-3, ISBN 13: 978-1-4405-0392-4 and *The Everything® Parent's Guide to Raising Mindful Children* by Jeremy Wardle and Maureen Weinhardt, copyright © 2013 by F+W Media, Inc., ISBN 10: 1-4405-6130-3, ISBN 13: 978-1-4405-6130-6.

ISBN 10: 1-4405-9417-1

ISBN 13: 978-1-4405-9417-5

eISBN 10: 1-4405-9418-X

eISBN 13: 978-1-4405-9418-2

Printed in the United States of America.

10   9   8   7   6   5   4   3   2   1

Cover design by Frank Rivera.

This book is available at quantity discounts for bulk purchases.
For information, please call 1-800-289-0963.

Dedication

This book is dedicated to all the children with autism who have given my life deep purpose and rich meaning.

Acknowledgments

Thank you to: Cliff Burnett, autism miracle worker who has taught me so much about how to truly care for and reach people with autism. Kevin Bailey, business partner extraordinaire, who makes work great fun and always has the most brilliant direction on how to truly reach parents and professionals. Paul Washington, who always believes in me.

Contents

Introduction

If you are the parent of a child on the autism spectrum, you may sometimes feel discouraged. You aren't alone. This book will provide you with many practical solutions to seemingly insurmountable challenges, plus advice on how to handle family and community difficulties and how to deal with your own thoughts and feelings so that you can enjoy life.

The diagnosis of autism, though it may not feel this way at times, can open up a whole new world for you and your family. Many brilliant people have been diagnosed with autism and have done amazing things. There are many children with autism who are able to go to college and become successful leaders in their field. To help you deal with your frustrations, it is important to remember to find a balance of both accepting your child and learning how to teach him to grow beyond the limitations of his condition.

As a parent, you are an important part of the team that will help your child thrive. It is particularly important to find autism experts who can accurately guide you through the diagnostic process and the labyrinth of treatments. Networking with other parents may help you find the right professionals to be part of your team of experts. It may take time and effort to find the right professionals to care for your child, but it is worth the legwork so that you feel supported and validated, and confident that your child is receiving the correct treatment to meet your family's needs.

If your first visit to a physician or any professional leaves you feeling uncomfortable or inadequate, please keep looking. Individuals who have compassion and wisdom, are supportive, and understand the needs of your child and family can help make your journey a bit easier. When it comes to your child, you are truly the expert. An effective professional learns things from you, as you learn from her.

There is much involved in raising children who are not on the autism spectrum, and the needs amplify when there is a child with special needs. May this book support you so that you can learn how to pay attention to your child and at the same time care for yourself, your partner, and your other children. The tips and solutions in this book can help keep your life in balance. Along with learning how to effectively handle the challenges involved with autism, may you also discover how your child can profoundly touch your heart and impact your life in many amazing and unexpected ways.

An important note:

After a great deal of consideration, throughout this book the author has chosen to use the terms "child with autism" and "person with autism" to describe those on the autism spectrum. However, the author and publisher acknowledge the ongoing debate as to how to refer to people on the spectrum: "He or she is autistic" or "He or she has autism." Parents, professionals, and people with autism may have different preferences regarding these important semantic disagreements. Ultimately, the author and publisher wish to respect the individual wishes of those on the spectrum, and urge readers first to get to know an individual and his or her preferences before choosing terms.

 **CHAPTER 1**

Conscious Parenting

Being a conscious parent is all about building strong, sustainable bonds with your children through mindful living and awareness. Traditional power-based parenting techniques that promote compliance and obedience can disconnect you from your children. Conscious parenting, on the other hand, helps you develop a positive emotional connection with your child. You acknowledge your child's unique self and attempt to empathize with her way of viewing the world. Through empathetic understanding and tolerance you create a safe environment where your child feels that her ideas and concerns are truly being heard. When you find yourself in a stressful situation with your child, rather than reacting with anger or sarcasm, conscious parenting reminds you to take a step back, reflect, and look for a peaceful solution—one that honors your child's individuality and motivations. This approach benefits all children, especially children with autism, as they experience the world differently, and often are overwhelmed by sensory issues. Adopting the conscious parenting philosophy can relieve your stress and improve your child's self-image. The strong bond built between you and your child, along with your own calm, respectful attitude, can help her to develop positive behavior patterns.

The Benefits of Conscious Parenting

Conscious parenting isn't a set of rules or regulations that you must follow, but rather a system of beliefs. Conscious parents engage and connect with their children using mindful and positive discipline rather than punishment. They try to be present when they're spending time with their children, avoiding distractions such as TV and social media. Conscious parents respect their children and accept them as they are. The most important part of conscious parenting is building an emotional connection with your child so you can understand the underlying reasons for her behavior.

Conscious parenting does not exclude setting boundaries, but it does give children respect. It's not that they can do whatever they want; age-appropriate boundaries are extremely important, especially if your children are very young or have special needs. Many parents are very busy with life's demands. There becomes little time to simply relax and enjoy each other. Conscious parenting principles help you understand how to have a balance between doing and being and how this impacts the peace in your household.

Understanding conscious parenting principles and applying mindfulness principles can help you raise your self-awareness and show you different ways to deal directly with thoughts and feelings that emerge from your role as a parent. Mindfulness is a powerful way to develop awareness, and is a practical tool for working with thoughts or feelings instead of ignoring them or getting swept away by them. Mindfulness helps you to practice being present within your life, just as it is, and to be more intentional about what you do as a result. As you learn new ways to pay attention, you can be more of the parent you want to be.

Mindfulness is the practice of being attentive in every moment, and noticing what is taking place both inside and outside of you without passing judgment. It is the practice of purposefully seeing your thoughts, emotions, experiences, and surroundings as they arise. Simply put, mindfulness is the act of paying attention.

Conscious parenting involves understanding your child's behavior, monitoring and modifying your own behavior, and making conscious choices as to how you react and offer consequences and boundaries. When you understand how your child experiences the world and how she learns, you can communicate in ways that really reach her.

Self-Awareness and Self-Control

One of the first things you learn with conscious parenting is how to pay attention to yourself and the rise of different thoughts and feelings in your own mind. The simple act of noticing that a feeling is coming on or that a particular idea has come up can be a powerfully liberating experience.

When you first start focusing on your awareness, you may not notice that a thought or feeling has taken hold of you until you are in the middle of acting (or after the fact). As you become more acquainted with the practice, you will find it easier to notice the movements of your mind as they happen, rather than catching yourself "red-handed" in the middle of an emotional reaction or outburst (or after it has already passed). You will also start to notice the things that tend to set you off—your triggers—and you will begin to be able to anticipate your emotions before they have a hold on you.

PAYING ATTENTION

Attention and awareness can be powerful tools when addressing behavioral issues with your child. As you become more skilled at noticing the thoughts and feelings that arise, you will begin to notice them more quickly, maybe even before they start to affect your actions. This awareness opens up the possibility to say "Hey, I'm pretty mad right now . . . " instead of yelling at somebody you care about because you were upset about something else. The practice can do exactly the same thing for your children, helping them learn to communicate about their feelings rather than just react from that place of emotion.

Often, you may notice that your emotions carry with them a sense of urgency. As you feel the impulse to do something arise within you, you will be able to see the forces driving that sense of "I need to do something." They could be, for example, the thoughts that come up as you watch your child put on her own shoes. Your mind might be buzzing with impatience, and the thought "I need to put her shoes on for her because she's taking forever" arises. When you notice this thought, rather than immediately acting on it you have some room to pause, check in with yourself, and act intentionally instead of reacting. This practice of noticing creates a certain amount of mental space so you can deal with a thought or feeling rather than being moved to act by it.

Because of their severe state of anxiety, people with autism may find that what is bearable to others is completely intolerable to them. Do not baby your child, but calm her and encourage her to move on. She will feel your strength and encouragement and eventually regroup.

Empathy and Communication

As you become more aware of yourself and how you are responding to your environment, it becomes possible to apply this awareness to your communication with others. Noticing your thoughts and feelings can allow you to express yourself more intentionally, which can lead to more satisfying communication with others. When applied to what you notice about others, mindfulness can help you to express your perceptions or observations before reacting negatively (e.g., asking "You look/sound upset; is everything okay?" before reacting based on an assumption).

CREATING CONNECTIONS

These skills can be used to connect with your child as well. Whenever you see your child, truly look at her and acknowledge her. Slow yourself down and gently touch her; you may be surprised to see that she will give you some eye contact! Children with autism are very sensitive to others' moods. When they feel that you are calm and loving, they will feel that you are safe and begin to meet you halfway, no matter their IQ. Smile at them and be happy to see them. They will lighten up and respond to you.

As you notice your own thoughts and feelings, moment by moment, you will come to better understand what gives rise to those feelings. Although there is rarely a concrete or simple answer as to why you feel a particular way, you will begin to understand the many complex factors that influence your feelings and your behavior. Because other people function much like you do, you may find over time that you can respond more compassionately and actually defuse situations.

Interact and talk with your children in simple, straightforward ways. You can ask, "I'm so happy to see you. How are you doing today? Are you okay?" If you demonstrate that you care about them when they are not upset, it will be much easier to calm them when they become distraught.

Engaged Listening

Listening is one of the most important skills in your parenting toolbox. It is an important way to support your child and demonstrate that you care. Listening is a tricky concept because it is not immediately obvious what you actually do when you listen. Engaged listening, otherwise known as active listening, is a process by which you give someone else your complete attention. With nonverbal children with autism, there may not be as much conversation, as you are observing and tuning into their body language, facial expressions, and breathing patterns and to the sounds they are making.

SETTING DISTRACTIONS ASIDE

All too often people multitask their way through the day. This is a coping mechanism you may have developed as a means of juggling the many projects, tasks, errands, and obligations that you are responsible for. It splits your attention in ways that distract your mind and lessen the quality of your engagement, which can cause your work and social interactions to suffer.

To avoid this becoming an issue between you and your child (and to make sure you're modeling the kind of focus and engagement you want your child to manifest in her own life), make sure to practice engaged listening when you are with your family. This means setting aside other distractions, making eye contact, and giving your child your full attention.

When you set down what you are doing and look at the person who is talking, check in with yourself. Is your mind focused on what the person is saying, or is it still planning, scheduling, remembering, projecting, or worrying? It is very easy to only half-listen, and this can be especially true when it comes to listening to children.

Here is a list of ways to hone your active listening skills during conversations:

O *Remove distractions and tune in.* It's impossible to really listen to what someone is saying when there are distractions in the background. Turn off the television or radio, stop what you are doing, and make it clear to the other person that the conversation is your top priority.

O *Pay attention to the person speaking.* Engaged listeners provide many clues that they are paying attention. Eye contact is important, and demonstrates to the person speaking that you are right there with her. Even if your child does not give you eye contact, it is fine for you to look at her, as she will sense that you are paying attention to her.

O *Connect with the speaker.* Even if the content of the conversation is not initially interesting, remind yourself that you care about the person talking. Use that as your gateway to caring about the content. Think to yourself, "I care about you. What you're talking about is important to you, and I like that you are inviting me into your world." You may be surprised how positively she will respond to your thoughts!

○ *If your child is verbal, ask clarifying and reflecting questions.* These are great ways to show that you are engaged with the subject matter. Repeat/reflect different points to make sure you understand (e.g., "So wait, if I'm hearing you right . . . "), or when appropriate ask questions that expand the topic or invite different perspectives (e.g., "What do you think about . . . ").

○ *Listen, don't plan.* Often in conversations, people are simply waiting for their turn to talk. This is the opposite of listening. Although it is tempting to formulate responses in your mind, hold that impulse at bay until the other person is finished talking.

○ *Be aware of your mind.* Thoughts have a tendency to wander, and are often sparked by the topic of conversation at hand. When you notice your mind wandering, gently turn your attention back to the speaker. Just as in meditation when you notice thoughts arising and refocus on your breath, you can notice your mind beginning to wander during a conversation and bring your focus back to the speaker. You can apply your core practice during conversations with others and you may find that the conversation goes more smoothly. A core practice is a technique that you can do frequently throughout your day to calm yourself when you are in a stressful situation. This practice takes you out of habitual reactions so you can develop new positive habits and parent more effectively.

Engaged listening is another way to show how much you love and support your child by making her a priority and demonstrating that you care about her.

Understanding Behavior

Conscious parenting and mindfulness can help you to stay calm and aware when dealing with a strong emotional response from your child. Mindful listening can be a helpful tool for practicing compassion, and may allow you to respond to rudeness with kindness instead of reacting with mirrored rudeness or insensitivity.

- Take a moment to breathe, slow yourself down, and calm yourself.

- Become aware of your own emotions in response to your child's reactions. Do you become agitated, stressed, or impatient? What happens to your body when your child starts to escalate?

- Reclaim a calm state by taking three deep breaths and notice your own emotional reactions before you react to your child.

- Notice what happens to your child when she becomes upset. Does she shake, cry, or collapse? Simply observe her reactions.

- Acknowledge and validate any needs your child may be expressing. You may want to provide a sensory strategy or tell her calmly, "I'm here; you are safe." Do not try to reason with her, argue with her, or tell her to "calm down"; that will only make her more upset. When people are extremely emotional and in overload and you tell them to "calm down," it can make them feel even more anxious and agitated.

- Look for cues that she has calmed and regrouped. Look for relaxation in her speech or sounds and in her face and body, and wait for deep breathing to emerge.

- When she has fully calmed down, you can gently touch her arm, face, or shoulder and smile warmly. Do not speak out loud, but your touch and your smile will let her know nonverbally that everything is okay. Your smile and softness will help her re-integrate and become calm.

This process can help you create a deeper bond with your child. Children become more anxious when they feel afraid of a parent. As you let them know that you love them and they are safe, they will feel more relaxed and their ability to follow your directions and be less resistant will improve.

Parents who are uncomfortable with or do not know how to handle intense emotions will either walk away from, ignore, or lash out at a child. Learn to find ways to enjoy your child when she is not upset. If you are constantly tense and frustrated with your child, she will feel this. It creates a negative feedback loop, making her more upset and doubtful of your ability to care for her. Use your breathing and calming strategies so you can be reassuring and confident when you calm her.

Important Points to Consider

This chapter introduced you to the value of conscious parenting and mindfulness.

- Conscious parenting involves both treating your child with respect and offering firm, clear boundaries.

- Mindfulness is the practice of paying attention to how you use and direct your brain.

- A mindfulness practice helps you slow down so you can choose different behaviors instead of reacting unconsciously.

- You cannot expect your children to respond with respect and love if you cannot model and teach them these skills.

 **CHAPTER 2**

The World of Autism

When you start learning about autism spectrum disorder, you may feel as if you've entered into a new world, with an unfamiliar language, norms, and behaviors. The moment you receive the diagnosis that your child is on the autism spectrum, everything changes. While your first reaction might be fear, do not be discouraged. There will be disappointments and there will also be beautiful gifts that accompany his diagnosis. The good news is that this world can be navigated successfully, and the diagnosis can mark the beginning of a new adventure for you and your child.

What Is Autism Spectrum Disorder?

Autism spectrum disorder, often referred to as ASD, involves challenges with socialization, communication, motor skills, and information processing, as well as unusual responses to sensory input. No two children with autism display this condition in exactly the same way, so it is important to understand exactly how your child functions.

THE SIGNS AND SYMPTOMS OF AUTISM

Autism has specific signs and symptoms that vary in prominence among children with the condition. The diagnosis is made based on evaluation of symptoms and specific developmental tests.

Your child's physician will be involved in making the diagnosis, and a child psychologist or psychiatrist may also examine your child or do specific tests. Other experts will be consulted if needed. The professionals will look for the following signs and symptoms to determine the diagnosis:

- Expressive and receptive communication challenges
- Difficulties with socialization
- Insistence on routine and resistance to change
- Appearing to be "off in his own world"
- Resistance to physical closeness such as hugging, or extreme need for physical touch
- Attachment to "odd" objects such as toys, kitchen utensils, or string
- Parallel play—playing beside other children rather than interacting with them
- Lack of imaginative play
- Sudden anger and tantrums
- Repetitive and obsessive behaviors
- Hyper- or hyporeactivity to sensory input, or unusual interests in sensory aspects of the environment

- Difficulties with eye contact

- Difficulties with gross and fine motor skills

- Deficits in developing, maintaining, and understanding relationships

- Stereotyped or repetitive motor movements, use of objects, or speech

- Extreme distress over small changes

- Highly restricted, fixated interests

- Difficulty interpreting subtle cues, such as facial expression or tone of voice

- Repetitive, meaningless use of words

- Frustration due to inability to communicate his basic needs and wants

- Stimming: spinning, twirling, or twisting objects repeatedly

- Combining or alternating repetitive activities including rocking, flapping, and repeating words or phrases and other repetitive activities

- Unusual eye movements and vision habits

The diagnostic criteria for ASD changed in 2013 with the publication of the fifth edition of the *Diagnostic and Statistical Manual of Mental Disorders* (DSM-5). Asperger's Disorder, Pervasive Developmental Disorder Not Otherwise Specified (PDD-NOS), and Rett's Disorder were deleted and all diagnoses are now classified as Autism Spectrum Disorder. Under the new criteria, the evaluating doctor provides a diagnosis of both the condition and the severity of patient need. There are three levels of severity: Level 1, "Requiring support"; Level 2, "Requiring substantial support"; and Level 3, "Requiring very substantial support." These changes were made because many states were not providing insurance coverage for services for Asperger's Syndrome and PDD.

THE SUBTLE CUES OF COMMUNICATION

A lot of communication is based on unspoken cues, such as hand gestures, body language, eye movements, and even pauses in conversation. All of these convey emotions and messages that may be subtle but are crucial to understanding the meaning of what someone is saying. For a person with autism, who lives in a world where words have literal meanings, these nonverbal cues are so subtle that they are frequently missed. Difficulties with socialization are generally the most obvious symptom of autism.

It is possible for people with autism to learn social mannerisms by repetition, but they do not generally understand the meaning behind them, and consequently, socialization suffers. Often people will misunderstand what a person with autism is trying to say because his conversation is so literal. These misunderstandings can lead to hurt feelings and anger.

There are children who are extremely shy and take a long time to interact with other children. A child like this could be thought to have autism. The difference is that in time, shy children will begin to make friends and not insist on solitary play. They will play with others when they feel comfortable.

THE PROBLEM WITH CONCEPTUAL THINKING

Children with autism struggle profoundly with conceptual ideas and abstract thinking. They are very literal. For example, a child with autism may associate leaving the house with putting on a coat. Now imagine that same child outdoors without a coat on, and the temperature drops dramatically. Although the child might have a coat with him, even in his hands, he will not put it on. Why not? He associates the coat with leaving the house, not with a solution to cold weather, and the concept of using the coat for protection is nonexistent. The child also has difficulties recognizing that other people have their own thoughts, feelings, attitudes, and beliefs different from his own.

Not all children with autism display aggression, though it is very common. Fifty-three percent of the children diagnosed have severe outbursts. These can range from abrupt, brief explosions to full-fledged meltdowns. Children with autism may strike out by hitting, biting, kicking, flailing, or spitting, as well as by destroying objects and possessions.

AUTISM AND IQ

If a child is nonverbal and is unable to understand concepts, he will perform poorly on IQ tests. A score of eighty or below on an IQ test is considered a developmental delay. It is unlikely that a child with autism can be measured accurately using standardized IQ testing.

IQ stands for intelligence quotient. The Wechsler Intelligence Scale for Children, fourth edition (WISC-IV), is designed for children between the ages of six and sixteen. This assessment is commonly administered to children with autism because it can be completed without reading or writing.

A 2015 study by the Research Center of the Hôpital Rivière-des-Prairies showed that children with autism-related disorders are at risk of being underestimated using the WISC-IV. "Nonverbal" or "minimally verbal" children are at risk of being judged "low-functioning" or "untestable" via conventional cognitive testing practices. This test does not assess the children's true knowledge because it does not test autistic cognitive strengths; therefore, they may be incorrectly regarded as having little cognitive potential.

Related Spectrum Disorders

There are eight genetic disorders that can have features of autism but are caused by a genetic disorder. These include Angelman Syndrome, Asperger's Syndrome, Fragile X Syndrome, Landau-Kleffner Syndrome, Prader-Willi Syndrome, Rett Syndrome, tardive dyskinesia, and Williams Syndrome. Each disorder has its own specific symptoms, as well as symptoms commonly found in autism.

It is common for physicians and therapists not to commit to the diagnosis of autism or one of its cousins, saying instead that a child is "autistic-like." This is usually reluctance on the part of the physician to deliver a diagnosis. It can be difficult for a physician to tell parents that their child has a condition that will not disappear over time, and it can be extremely difficult for parents to accept such a diagnosis. The diagnosis of autism is a stigma for many families, and parents will often be in denial.

Obtaining a diagnosis of autism may be one of the greatest challenges that you, as a parent, will encounter. It will require you to develop new skills of mindfulness so that you can manage your own frustration and emotions and make the most effective decisions for your child and family. You will need to be assertive with professionals who may be reluctant to make such a diagnosis, or you may need to find a specialist if your current doctor is not qualified to recognize autism spectrum disorder (for example, if the symptoms are not dramatic, she may attribute them to the wrong behavioral or psychiatric disorder).

A diagnosis of autism can also cause a conflict between parents, with one parent accepting the diagnosis and wanting to start therapy immediately while the other is in denial and refuses to allow treatment. If you are in this situation, it would be beneficial to use your mindfulness practices so you can communicate more calmly with your partner.

Age of Onset

A decade ago, the incidence of autism was one in ten thousand children. It was a rare disorder, and few people had ever heard of it or met anyone who had it. In the recent past, however, the number of children diagnosed with autism has exponentially risen. Prevalence in the United States was estimated in 2014 at one in sixty-eight births.

The question remains whether the number is a true reflection of an actual increase of children with ASD or whether the procedures for diagnosis are simply more accurate now. Could it be that ASD is recognized and properly labeled more often because parents, teachers, pediatricians, and others who work with children have become better educated and more aware of autism and related conditions? Were children who had autism thirty years ago overlooked and therefore not treated?

If autism has not increased in numbers and it is simply being diagnosed more carefully and accurately now, where are all of the adults born forty or fifty years ago with autism who were undiagnosed as children?

What is known is that autism is not discriminating. It affects children of both sexes and all races and ethnic groups. Many children with autism display the diagnostic signs and symptoms between the ages of two and four. According to the American Academy of Pediatrics, children may begin to display the signs of autism between eighteen and twenty-four months. Although some children have qualities that concern their parents almost from birth, a child can develop normally up to about eighteen months and then begin to regress, losing skills already mastered, including speech, motor skills, socialization, and behavior. The website *www.firstsigns.org* is helpful if you have concerns about your child. Getting an early diagnosis means that early treatment and intervention are possible. Early intervention can make a huge difference in a child's future. If a child receives appropriate therapy and treatments beginning at approximately age two or three, the long-term outlook is much better. The future is also much brighter for the entire family.

Sometimes, even though they see their children day after day, parents may not recognize that their son or daughter is not reaching developmental milestones. This is where the extended family can help by alerting the parents about any issues they perceive with the child. Grandparents are often the ones to spot the delays and may be the first to point them out. Unfortunately, even if a grandparent realizes that a grandchild has a problem, the parents may not be convinced, and may do nothing until a teacher or physician insists that the child be tested.

COMMUNICATION

Human beings rely on communication to express their needs and get those needs met, to create connections, and to clarify information. The most painful challenge for most parents to understand and cope with on a day-to-day basis is the difficulties with communication.

A child may be suspected of being hearing impaired because of the total lack of response to spoken language. It is common for the diagnostic trail to begin with a parent or grandparent asking for a test because of the child's apparent lack of hearing. However, when the tests show that the child's hearing is normal, further testing can lead to the ASD diagnosis.

Your Emotional Reaction

When parents first absorb the information that their child is somewhere on the autism spectrum, they experience various stages of emotion as they cope with feelings of grief and loss. You will, too. There *has* been a loss—a loss of dreams, potential, and hopes for a future that will now be different from any you could have anticipated. You may experience guilt, denial, hopelessness, depression, sadness, anger, desperation, and any number of other emotional reactions. Any or all of these reactions can be expected when you receive a diagnosis for your child.

LOSS OF DREAMS

When a couple learns of a pregnancy, it is almost impossible not to have expectations for the infant growing in the mother's womb. It is also natural to project dreams of this child's future: playing baseball, camping, marching in the school band . . . the list of possibilities is as varied as the families into which the children are born.

When a child is diagnosed with a disability, so many of the preconceived notions of what life could have been like for this child are lost. The feeling of loss is tremendous and can be a devastating blow to parents. The imagined arguments over curfews, borrowing the car, going to college, and bringing home a girlfriend or boyfriend for the first time become anticipated events that just slip away from the future like water through open fingers. This loss of dreams is not unlike a death, and hopes and dreams for the future have to be reevaluated.

GUILT

Parents invariably turn inward when something goes wrong with their child. It is a natural reaction. As a mother, you may question every aspect of your pregnancy and wonder what you did to cause the autism or what you could have done to prevent it. You may look in the mirror and analyze every moment in an effort to determine what you did wrong to cause this to happen to your child. As a father, you may also turn inward as you find ways to blame yourself for what has happened—even going so far as to despise yourself for some perceived or imagined wrong.

It is important to understand that ASD is not caused by parental neglect. It is not your fault. It is even more important for health care providers to realize that parents are going through this grieving process.

DENIAL

When a situation arises that exceeds a person's ability to cope, such as a diagnosed illness that requires extensive support and care, denial is often the result. It is human nature to handle a devastating situation by simply pretending it does not exist. This is not a failure to "handle it" on the part of the person. In many ways, it shows that the coping mechanisms are functioning normally in the part of the human brain that allows only a certain amount of stress to be processed at a time. By avoiding a stress overload, the ability to cope is maintained.

Feeling guilt can have the same effects as undergoing excessive stress. Headaches, depression, and other physical and emotional symptoms may be experienced, and sometimes people turn to overeating or substance abuse in an attempt to remove the pain. If you are feeling this level of stress, you may want to consider counseling so that you can receive support and know that you are not alone.

If one or both parents remain in denial, it is important to seek intervention through some form of counseling. Counseling can help a person understand that while the disability does change a parent's life, it is not the end of your world, although it may feel that way in the beginning.

Everyone has to cope in her own way. For some, acceptance comes quickly; for others, it is a lengthy process. There is no right or wrong way to do this. Learning to deal with the diagnosis of autism has to be done at your own pace.

HOPELESSNESS

Your ability to deal with the diagnosis of autism will wax and wane. At times you will feel you can handle just about anything; at other times you will feel totally helpless to protect and assist your child. Both of these reactions are very normal. There will be many times when you can't make life easier for your child, and feelings of hopelessness will be natural at such times. This is where your mindfulness practice will be very helpful to help you calm yourself and regain perspective.

Many parents look at a child's entire life and, in one day, try to solve all the problems they foresee their child facing. This can amplify your feelings of hopelessness and may overwhelm you. It is normal to experience feelings of hopelessness when you cannot easily solve the problems your child faces. Try your mindfulness practice and see if slowing down and taking three deep breaths can help you start to slowly shift your perspective.

Having a counselor whom you feel safe with and trust can also help you regain perspective and hope.

ANGER

Hearing that a child has a lifelong condition with an unknown cause for which there is no absolute and effective treatment is enough to make anyone angry. Anger is a normal part of the grief process. However, some parents stay stuck in anger long-term and this profoundly impacts the child. When any child lives in an environment where there is long-term and excessive negativity, they will feel this and act it out. There is so much frustration that a child with autism feels already by the nature of his challenges that also having to deal with the parents' long-term feelings can cause him to retreat even more into his own world. It is necessary for the growth of your family for you to have healthy ways to process and move on from your anger over time.

It is only natural to be infuriated by a situation that is out of your control. Talking it over with a therapist or trusted friend can be very helpful. Meeting other parents who are dealing with the same challenges is also helpful. Support groups are available all over the world. Surrounding yourself with people who also have children with autism will help the anger dissipate into actions that are more constructive.

DESPERATION

This is one of the most common reactions; virtually all parents will experience this emotion. There are many parents of newly, and not so newly, diagnosed children who will do or try just about anything to "cure" ASD. Many spend hours of research on the Internet, in libraries, in public records, or in private book collections to find the one thing that may "fix" their child's autism. It is not unusual to find a parent spending six to eight hours each day on the Internet exploring new treatments.

It is important that parents recognize their vulnerability in this area. A tantalizing product that may cure your child is hard to resist, and the hunt for one might seem a worthwhile use of time. But keep in mind that you need to meet all of your family members' needs for time and attention, and you should avoid letting wishful thinking cloud your ability to determine whether what you are being offered is viable and ethical.

Possible Causes

To understand why there is such general disagreement regarding the possible causes of autism, it must be understood that there are some very controversial issues behind autism spectrum disorder. There are many theories and conflicts over causes, including vaccinations, genetics, contamination of the brain and body by heavy metals, disease processes, diets, and allergies. Many feel there is no one single cause but that a combination of triggers, combined in a unique way, has caused a cascade effect resulting in the condition called autism.

NEURO-IMMUNE DYSFUNCTION SYNDROME (NIDS)/ AUTOIMMUNE DISEASE

Interestingly enough, when the number of autism-related disorders in the population began to increase, so did the incidences of autoimmune diseases and chronic fatigue syndrome (CFS), as well as attention deficit disorders (ADD/ADHD). It is common to find a family in which one parent suffers from CFS or another autoimmune disorder, an older child has ADD, and a younger child falls somewhere on the autism spectrum.

The NIDS theory says that many, if not most, patients who suffer from a variety of autoimmune disorders, as well as autism, actually have a neuro-immune dysfunction. This causes chemical imbalances, which subsequently cause a restriction in the blood flow to the brain. In autism, the area of the brain affected would be the area controlling speech, language, socialization, and obsessive behaviors. The trigger for these changes could be environmental, or an illness.

If this theory holds true, then we're dealing with a new disease that has a great potential for treatment. This theory has not yet been proved, but physicians researching NIDS and the treatment of it are seeking to modify or eliminate the symptoms of autism in their patients.

VACCINATIONS

There is extensive controversy regarding the link between vaccinations and autism. Some believe that there is no link between vaccines and autism, while others believe there is. It was reported by the National Consumers League in April 2014 that one in four parents link autism to vaccinations and one in eight parents say they refused at least one vaccination. For more information, see *www.nclnet.org/survey_one_third_ of_american_parents_mistakenly_link_vaccines_to_autism*.

If a parent chooses not to have a child immunized, upon entering school a religious exemption may be claimed or a letter can be presented from the child's physician stating that he believes vaccinations would be harmful to the child's health and should not be given.

GENETICS

Many people believe that the cause of autism spectrum disorder will be found to have a genetic basis. The completion of the Human Genome Project will accelerate this line of research. The fact that many families with one child with autism will later have one or more on the autism spectrum has led many to believe that autism "runs" in families. However, the only autism spectrum disorders that have conclusively been proved to be genetic are Fragile X Syndrome and Rett Syndrome. Both of those disorders can be documented by blood work that looks directly at the chromosomes involved, and the genetic mutation can be identified.

There appears to be a genetic basis for some cases of autism. In families with one child diagnosed with autism, there is a 3 to 9 percent chance of a second child being diagnosed as autistic, and a 30 percent greater possibility of identical twins being autistic as compared with fraternal twins.

ENVIRONMENTAL CAUSES

Another theory that either stands alone or works in conjunction with other theories is that environmental issues may cause autism. The world is now inundated with pollution, wi-fi, processed food, and toxic elements that were not present in past eras and that can impact the health and well-being of our children.

Research is being done; however, at this time, no one has been able to determine a single cause of autism and many believe that the causes are multifaceted. There are federal plans to invest $165 million to expand and integrate existing studies on environmental influences. For more information, go to *www.autismspeaks.org/science/science-news/ nih-revives-study-environmental-risks-autism-and-other-childhood-disorders.*

It is important for parents of any child with an unusual condition or disability to learn how to regain their perspective when they become worried. If you find yourself becoming excessively concerned about the causes of your child's condition, try using your mindfulness practice to help you slow down, breathe, and calm yourself. This practice can help you re-focus on the present moment.

Important Points to Consider

Receiving the autism diagnosis can be very challenging to you as a parent. It will require you to reevaluate all your hopes, goals, and dreams for your child.

- Children with ASD have problems with understanding subtle communication cues, emotional regulation, and conceptual thinking.

- The IQ tests commonly used for autism do not accurately show cognitive potential for children with ASD.

○ A mindfulness practice can help you manage your frustrations and emotions so that you can make effective decisions for your child and family.

○ Your emotional reactions to the diagnosis may involve grief over the loss of dreams, guilt, denial, anger, desperation, and hopelessness.

○ There are many theories about the causes of autism. These include vaccinations, genetics, heavy metals, disease processes, diets, and allergies. Many feel there is no one single cause but that a combination of triggers results in the condition.

○ Parents can spend extensive time researching new treatments. Be sure that doing so does not cause you to neglect the emotional and financial needs of other family members.

 **CHAPTER 3**

Detecting Warning Signs and Coexisting Conditions

Children with autism often have coexisting conditions that, if left untreated, can increase their frustration and challenging behaviors. It's important for parents to understand a bit about these conditions so they can watch closely for symptoms that need medical attention, particularly if there are challenges with communication. Correctly treating these coexisting conditions will make a huge difference in the function and ease of your child's life. There are a multitude of coexisting conditions that can accompany autism. Your child may or may not have all of them, but a minimum of three to five of these conditions are typically present. Once you recognize any of these conditions, you can discuss your concerns with professionals.

Sensory Processing Disorder

The sensory system gives you information about your surroundings so you know how to properly respond to stimuli. Sensory processing disorder (SPD) occurs when there is hypersensitivity, hyposensitivity, or an unusual fascination with sensory stimuli. When the sensory and nervous systems are heightened, that makes it difficult for children with autism to correctly register and interpret sensory information. More than 90 percent of children with autism are reported to have atypical sensory behaviors.

The following list explains the functions of the sensory system and how they may be affected in your child.

○ The visual system (sight) is responsible for a person's sight and ability to detect light, darkness, and color. Many children with autism prefer to be in dark areas or cover themselves with blankets to block out the light as they experience discomfort or pain due to a physical sensitivity of the eyes. Allow for dim lighting in your home and have sunglasses handy for when your child is exposed to bright lights.

○ The auditory system (hearing) notifies us of danger and pleasure, connection, and general survival, even for people in modern times. It is common to see a child with autism suddenly cover her ears in an effort to block out all sound. One theory for this hypersensitivity is that people with autism do not discriminate sounds, but hear all sounds equally. If your child suddenly covers her ears and looks for a way to escape, make every effort to lower the sound level or remove her to a quieter place. Sensory overload is painful, and allowing the situation to continue may result in a meltdown.

○ The gustatory system (taste) is responsible for helping us detect whether something is pleasurable or offensive and encourages us to consume food. Some of the taste buds of a child with autism may be diminished while other taste buds are extremely heightened. Many food restrictions are caused by an extreme aversion to textures and tastes.

○ The olfactory system (smell) affects emotions, food selection, and behavioral responses. Some children with autism will have a heightened sense of smell and others a diminished ability to discern odors. Some of these children may be able to use their sense of smell to help them become calm by smelling essential oils, while others may find the scents repulsive or have difficulty registering the odor.

○ The tactile system (touch) helps a person to feel sensations such as pressure, pain, and temperature. It is common for children with autism to have abnormal reactions to sensations, such as the inability to feel pain or an intolerance to heat or cold. Children with autism often prefer a firm pressure. Because of their heightened responses, light touch can aggravate them. Deep touch pressure is the type of surface pressure that is exerted in most types of firm touching, holding, and stroking. In contrast, light touch pressure is a superficial stimulation of the skin such as tickling, which can actually move the hairs on the skin. Occupational therapists have noted that a light touch alerts the nervous system, but deep pressure is relaxing and calming. Deep pressure techniques like giving your child a bear hug, brushing using the Wilbarger protocol, swinging in a lycra swing, and wearing weighted vests are all great options to provide calming.

○ The proprioceptive system, located in the brain and in the vestibular system of the inner ear, gives us cues on how to move our bodies in a smooth and coordinated manner. This information is necessary to properly register sensory information. It helps us know where our bodies are in space and how they are moving. When these systems are not working properly, a person can feel anxious and unbalanced.

To perform daily life tasks with ease, an intact sensory system is essential. Many children with autism present with overreactive, underreactive, or fluctuating levels of reactivity to sensory input that significantly impairs their ability to interact with others and with the environment. (See M. O'Neill and R.S. Jones, "Sensory-Perceptual Abnormalities in Autism: A Case for More Research?" *Journal of Autism and Developmental Disorders*, June 1997.)

ADHD and OCD

Children with ADHD (attention deficit hyperactivity disorder) display a range of behavioral symptoms such as poor concentration, hyperactivity, and impulsivity. As you will see, many of the features of ADHD are also found in autism.

O Cannot talk or play quietly; disruptive of others

O Difficulties waiting to take turns

O Does not seem to listen

O Has temper tantrums

O Oblivious to consequences

O Difficulties accepting soothing or being held

O Always on the move

ADHD in children with autism can be caused by anxiety and nervousness, the heightened sensory system, and difficulties understanding social rules and expectations.

Some parents use medications or natural supplements to help provide calming and focus for their child. Behavioral management strategies that teach a child how to sit and focus can also be taught.

OCD (obsessive-compulsive disorder) is a psychiatric disorder characterized by obsessive thoughts and compulsive behavior. It is a separate disorder from autism; however, everyone on the autism spectrum shows some degree of OCD. OCD symptoms can be quite debilitating, as the obsessions and compulsions can interfere with a person's daily activities because of the amount of time they involve. If a person with OCD is not allowed to perform the behaviors, he can experience severe anxiety. OCD involves:

O Recurring and persistent thoughts and images

O Persistent worry resulting from the thoughts and images

O Behaviors such as counting, hand washing, or any number of activities done repetitively

- Narrow food preference, often based on color or shape

- Lining up objects, such as trains, blocks, cars, or DVDs

- Opening or closing doors on cupboards or closets, or doors to the outside

- Spinning in circles or walking in a circle

- Stimming and flapping

- Rocking the body back and forth

- Counting objects repeatedly for no apparent reason

- Hiding or hoarding objects

- Preoccupation with objects being placed in a chosen location

- Gestures and facial movements that resemble Tourette Syndrome

If your child is diagnosed as having OCD and is not diagnosed on the autism spectrum, it is important that you seek a second opinion if you feel autism may be a possibility. Don't hesitate to follow your own instincts regarding your child's health. A pediatric neurologist, developmental pediatrician, or child psychologist familiar with autism are all resources that you should consider.

Visual Processing Disorder and Motor Problems

The brain, not the eyes, processes the visual information that we see, including things like symbols, pictures, and distances. Weakness in the visual cortex of the brain causes difficulties processing and interpreting what the eyes see.

Parents generally will look for vision problems by observing how their child watches television, colors pictures in a coloring book, or gauges distance while playing. Most children with autism have some kind of visual problem. Common indications for visual difficulties include:

- Difficulty maintaining visual contact with an object or person

- Challenges differentiating between the size, shape, and color of objects

- Confusing the meanings of written symbols such as those used in calculations

- Misjudging distance

- Experiencing poor spatial awareness, often resulting in frequent falls or bumping into objects despite normal vision tests

Visual abnormalities in children with autism can cause a total distortion in how they view the world and process that information. It can give a child the feeling that objects bounce or swim, jump unpredictably, are fragmented into tiny pieces, or are overly large. Poor visual processing can contribute to problems with fine motor skills, attention, focus, and in social interactions.

Vision therapy is a specialized area of eye care. The specialists who practice in this field are known as developmental optometrists. These doctors perform vision exams and check for particular vision conditions. They can prescribe therapies to improve vision and sensory integration skills.

DYSPRAXIA AND MOTOR CHALLENGES

A common problem in autism is compromised motor skills. These include difficulties with fine motor skills such as grasping objects, using utensils, handwriting, buttoning and fastening, and picking up small objects. Gross motor challenges include difficulties moving around with ease, throwing and kicking a ball, climbing, and walking without stumbling. These difficulties are compounded by the child's poor visual processing, which impacts her ability to see and perform basic activities.

Indictors of motor deficits include:

○ Low muscle tone or hypotonia

○ Delayed motor milestones including rolling, sitting, crawling, and walking

○ Coordination issues

○ Clumsiness and poor balance

○ Poor posture and core strength

○ Toe walking

An occupational therapist can work with your child to improve her motor skills. Strength, flexibility, posture, motor control, motor planning, and sensory organization are all areas that can be treated.

Sleep Disorders

Most children have difficulty falling asleep or staying asleep. Temporary sleep difficulties are normal. However, many children with ASD have ongoing sleep-related difficulties. The number of families affected varies from study to study, but significant sleep problems can occur in 40 to 80 percent of children with autism. Sleep is a critical component of health. It is essential for growth, to restore our bodies and immunity, and to enhance memory and learning.

For children with autism, insufficient sleep appears to impact daytime behaviors, making challenging behaviors worse. In addition, sleeping difficulties for the child lead to diminished sleep for parents and siblings, adding to the stress of parenting and family life. No one functions at his best when he is sleep-deprived.

Causes of sleep disorders can include:

○ Disturbances in the child's circadian rhythm

○ Anxiety

- Difficulties relaxing due to heightened reactions to light, sound, and touch

- Challenges with the social cues associated with bedtime

- Distraction from toys or objects in the bedroom that leads to stimming

- Medical problems including sleep apnea, night terrors, reflux, allergies, or seizures

---

Routines that encourage sleep are important. For a child with autism, it can be helpful to create a visual schedule to inform and reassure her of the expected steps in the routine. Consider the activities that your child is doing before bedtime. Are these activities calming or stimulating?

Auditory Processing Disorders and Seizure Disorder

Children with this condition have difficulties processing what they hear because their ears and brain are not properly coordinating. There is interference in the way the brain recognizes and interprets sounds, especially speech. Signs of an auditory processing disorder (APD) include:

- Frequently asking "Huh?" or "What?" and often needing information repeated

- Difficulty following multistep directions

- Trouble understanding in noisy environments

- Poor memory for words and numbers

- Difficulties with focus and attention

- Trouble hearing the differences between sounds in words

O Difficulties remembering spoken information

O Challenges finding the right words to use

O Delayed verbal responses

O Misinterpreting questions and responding literally

O Becoming easily frustrated because of lack of understanding

Auditory processing disorders are common in children with autism. One theory says that the hippocampus in the brain, which is responsible for processing auditory information, may be underdeveloped in people with autism.

According to studies at the Children's Hospital of Philadelphia, another possibility could be that children with autism are hearing normally, but are processing sound more slowly than children without autism.

Guy Berard developed auditory integration training (AIT) in the 1960s to help people with auditory processing problems. Other similar training programs available are the Tomatis Method, Earobics, and Fast ForWord.

SEIZURE DISORDER

A seizure disorder is a medical condition characterized by episodes of uncontrolled electrical activity in the brain (seizures).

Of all the conditions that can occur with autism, perhaps none is as disconcerting to parents as seizures. Parents may feel out of control and fearful if their child has seizures. Twenty to 30 percent of children with autism have seizures, and one in four persons with autism begin to have seizures during puberty.

There are six types of seizures. The types and their characteristic signs are:

O Absence seizures, which involve a brief lapse of consciousness with a blank stare

O Atonic seizures, which have a loss of muscle tone

- Clonic seizures, which have repetitive jerking movements
- Myoclonic seizures, which involve sporadic jerking movements
- Tonic seizures, which have muscle stiffness and rigidity
- Grand mal seizures, which include unconsciousness, convulsions, and muscle rigidity

---

Parents and caretakers must know what to do if a seizure occurs. Dangerous objects need to be removed from the area and the adult should check that the child's airway is clear and no food or any object is stuck in her throat.

Depression, Bipolar Disorder, and Tourette Syndrome

DEPRESSION

Depression is a mood disorder characterized by extreme sadness and despair. It can have serious negative effects on health, relationships, and daily functioning.

Depression may occur in children with autism, especially in older children with high-functioning autism, because of the sense of isolation and frustration that accompanies their social and emotional issues. The symptoms of depression can include many or all of the following: flat emotional reactions and irritability; changes in thinking patterns; sleep disturbance; loss of interest in or withdrawal from family, friends, or outside activities; loss of energy; decreased appetite; and little interest in personal appearance.

Anxiety is extremely prevalent in autism. It is a generalized feeling of worry, nervousness, or unease about an imminent event or something with an uncertain outcome. Anxiety is explored in further detail in Chapter 4.

There are treatment options available, including appropriate medications, counseling, or a good support group. Some individuals benefit from exercise and dietary changes. If private therapy is not financially possible, some community clinics and teaching hospitals offer therapy.

BIPOLAR DISORDER

Bipolar disorder is a psychiatric disorder characterized by periods of elevated mood and periods of depression. An individual with bipolar disorder has moods that swing from one extreme to the other. This disorder is being diagnosed more frequently, either because the condition is more known, and therefore easier to diagnose, or because of other unknown factors.

Some children with autism have bipolar-like symptoms such as being hyperactive, talking rapidly, or repeatedly changing from subject to subject. These symptoms may not necessarily indicate bipolar disorder; however, rapid mood swings in any child should always be brought to the attention of a child psychiatrist who can make the diagnosis.

Some of the new medications used to treat this disorder can be extremely effective in controlling these mood swings. However, no child or teen should be started on medication without a complete physical examination, basic blood tests including a complete blood count, and a thyroid panel. A urinalysis should also be part of the diagnostic testing.

TOURETTE SYNDROME

Tourette Syndrome, when associated with autism, is a neurological disorder characterized by sudden, involuntary movements or vocal utterances known as tics. The exact cause of Tourette Syndrome is unknown, but both genetic and environmental factors are involved. Typical age of onset is from five to seven.

The most common tics seen in autism are eye blinking, facial movements, sniffing, and throat clearing. Tics present frequently in the midline of the body including the head, neck, and face. This is contrasted with the stereotyped movements of ASD, which have an earlier age of onset, are more symmetrical, rhythmical, and bilateral, and involve the extremities (e.g., flapping the hands).

Coprolalia is involuntary swearing or the involuntary utterance of obscene words or socially inappropriate and derogatory remarks. Coprolalia is rarely seen in autism because of the challenges with language and verbalization; you will more commonly see motor and vocal tics.

Intellectual Concerns

Intellectual disability is characterized by significant limitations in both intellectual functioning and in adaptive behavior, which covers many everyday social and practical skills. This disability originates before the age of 18. Approximately 75 percent of people with autism have an IQ below 70. It can be difficult to distinguish cognitive delays in children with autism because of their difficulties performing on demand. As mentioned previously, children with ASD are at risk of being grossly underestimated using standardized IQ tests.

Common symptoms of intellectual disability include:

O Difficulties speaking

O Challenges with memory

O Uncertainty with cause and effect

O Difficulties understanding social norms

O Difficulties thinking logically and problem solving

Effective structure, communication systems, rules, and systems are very helpful for children with cognitive delays.

Most people have difficulties focusing on tasks that are boring or repetitive, but children with cognitive delays require schoolwork and activities that will significantly peak their interest to keep them fully engaged. Because these children have significant difficulties focusing, it is very difficult to force them to pay attention. Offering them engaging work, simple but effective memory strategies, and matching the tasks to their abilities, not over their head or too simple for them, ensures their participation.

Physicality

Any of the physical issues that may occur in a child, including the usual childhood diseases, are just as likely to occur in the child with ASD. Migraines, allergies, scoliosis, and any number of disorders occur just as frequently in children with autism. It may be harder for a parent to determine the degree of illness, or even if it exists, because of the communication difficulties and the atypical reaction to pain in the child with autism, but time and experience will teach parents how to resolve these difficulties.

The most important thing a parent can remember is that not all of this will happen at once, and not all of it has to be solved immediately. It is a matter of discovering the issues, determining the best course of action, and then beginning to walk the path one step at a time to help your child with autism to become the happiest person possible.

Hearing Impairments

Hearing loss is a reduction or defect in the ability to perceive sound. Hearing losses may be discovered more quickly in a child with ASD because the child's early lack of communication or failure to respond may lead the parent to wonder if the child is hearing impaired.

It is normal for children to turn their heads to acknowledge their name or to look in the direction of a voice or an interesting sound. Children with autism do not always respond to voice, and this may be your first sign that "something is wrong." It is common for parents and grandparents who see this behavior to question whether or not the child can hear. If you are alerted to this behavior, the first thing to do is arrange to have the child's hearing tested by a qualified specialist.

Frequent ear infections that are not properly treated can lead to hearing loss. If a physician repeatedly prescribes antibiotics for ongoing ear infections, it would be wise to check with a pediatric ear, nose, and throat doctor. A procedure to release infection may be needed to prevent hearing loss.

THE IMPORTANCE OF EARLY DIAGNOSIS WITH HEARING LOSS

It may be difficult for the parents of a deaf child with autism to get an early diagnosis because of the challenge involved in recognizing the symptoms of autism, which are often masked by the hearing impairment. If you have a child with a hearing impairment and recognize many of the symptoms of autism, it is very important to have an evaluation done to determine if autism is also present. Early intervention and therapy is critical, and therapy can be initiated for both the hearing loss and the autism.

As the parent of a child with autism, you need to be especially mindful that your child may be watching you at any time. You can use these times to teach your child the activities of daily living, but be aware that she may also see things that could be harmful if misunderstood or imitated. For instance, she may not understand that alcohol is inappropriate for a child, so be careful about drinking in front of her and also keeping alcohol readily available in the house. Be mindful of how you greet and interact with your spouse, family members, or friends. Your child will notice how you treat people and model your actions accordingly. Remember, children do not adhere to the rule of "do what I say, not do what I do." Most children *will* do what you do, so try and model positive behaviors.

Hearing tests are very accurate, even on very young children. If it is determined that your child has a hearing deficit, the next step will be to determine what kind of deafness is occurring and how to treat it. If a child has a hearing loss, whether total or partial, it is important to intervene with the appropriate hearing aids, even if the child is completely nonverbal. Speech therapy is an important part of the treatment for a child with ASD, but the child must hear properly to learn to integrate speech into her life. If she has difficulty hearing, it will be even more difficult to compensate for the lack of speech.

If your child has a hearing loss as well as autism, you should understand that there will be progress. The challenges will be great, but the victories will be greater. If you are using sign language and are discouraged because you believe your child never looks at you, remember that people with ASD visualize in different ways. Your child may have been watching you in her peripheral vision and learned more than you realized.

Gastrointestinal and Bowel Disorders

The gastrointestinal (GI) tract includes the esophagus, stomach, small intestine, large intestine and rectum, liver, gallbladder, and pancreas. Meta-analysis of 15 studies from 1980–2012 indicates ASD children experience GI symptoms, food allergies, poor digestion, or malabsorption issues at a much higher rate than children without ASD (*http://pediatrics .aappublications.org/content/133/5/872.short*).

SIGNS OF A LEAKY GUT

O Digestive issues such as gas, bloating, diarrhea, or irritable bowel syndrome (IBS)

O Seasonal allergies or asthma

- Mood and mind issues such as depression, anxiety, ADD, or ADHD

- Skin issues such as acne, rosacea, or eczema

- Food allergies or food intolerances

- Candida overgrowth

The gastrointestinal system is often referred to as your "second brain," and contains 100 million neurons—more than either your brain or your spinal cord!

Treatment of leaky gut has been proven to reduce some of the more challenging symptoms of ASD. Treatment for leaky gut using dietary solutions will be discussed in Chapter 16. If you are concerned that your child has leaky gut, please discuss this with your pediatrician. The IPT is a medical test that can determine if your child is experiencing leaky gut. Find out more about this test at *www.psychologytoday.com/blog/evolutionary-psychiatry/201104/diet-and-autism.*

Important Points to Consider

It's important for you to understand a bit about all of the co-exisiting conditions your child may experience in case they require medical attention. Also, co-existing conditions may arise at different times of development and once correctly treated, can contribute to the ease of your child's and your own life.

- Coexisting conditions can profoundly impact your child's feelings of frustration and amplify her challenging behaviors.

- When coexisting conditions are properly treated, you can see significant improvements in the function and ease of your child's life.

○ Your child may have all of the coexisting conditions, though commonly, a child will have three to five of these conditions.

○ It is important for you to understand a bit about each of these conditions so you can know what to look for. Notify your physician of your concerns so your child can receive proper treatment as soon as possible.

CHAPTER 4

Managing Challenging Behaviors with Empathy

You may be familiar with how challenging some autistic behaviors can be. Mindfulness is an effective tool when handling your reactions to these behaviors, such as showing empathy instead of anger. Having empathy for your child means both offering compassion and providing firm boundaries and structure for his development. This is true for all children, but children with autism particularly need firm boundaries because they can be quite headstrong. Responding to challenging behaviors with patience, empathy, and mindfulness will not only calm your child, slow these behaviors, and prevent them from recurring, but you will also be modeling strength and acceptance while validating your child's feelings. Reacting with mindfulness will show your child you believe in his potential, accept the issues he may have, and encourage him to develop as much as possible. It is valuable for you to learn effective behavior management skills when your child is very young. Being firm can be hard, as it takes a lot of energy and consistency, but it will make a huge difference in your child's skill acquisition, the peace in your household, and his ability to contribute to society.

Handling Behaviors with Mindfulness

This section will explore common challenging behaviors your child with autism may exhibit, and different options for how you can stay calm and effectively handle these situations with empathy and without losing your cool. In tense situations, your core practice will be very helpful in reminding you to slow down, breathe deeply, and manage your reactions. This, in turn, will help your child be able to regroup and calm himself as well.

UNDERSTANDING ANXIETY

Children with autism frequently experience anxiety. Anxiety is a generalized feeling of worry, nervousness, and unease. When your child has trouble communicating, has difficulty identifying feelings, and has trouble understanding social expectations, he may feel a chronic level of discomfort or anxiety. This state can be caused by imbalanced brain chemistry, genetics, or life experiences.

When your child is anxious, do you notice your own anxiety increasing? Consciously defusing your own anxiety in these situations will in turn help you to focus on your child and his needs, and will help you bring him back to a calm state. Try using your core practice when your child is anxious instead of trying to talk with him, as sometimes verbalizations can increase anxiety in your child. See if reducing your language and breathing calmly helps him begin to relax. If you and your child are having a hard time breathing because of the anxiety, gently breathe through a straw ten times. This is an easy way for you to breathe and calm down. Your calming actions and speech can help your child regain focus during a period of sensory overload. Sometimes providing a communication system that gives clear expectations of what will be occurring can help alleviate anxiety. Because children with ASD have difficulty understanding time, the communication system can help them understand sequencing of events. The more they can anticipate what will be happening, the calmer they will feel. This will prevent them from constantly interrupting the parent to find out what will be happening and when. This will allow the parents to relax because they can focus on the activities at hand rather than constantly redirecting the child.

How to create effective communication systems will be discussed in more detail in Chapter 5.

DEFUSING AGGRESSION AND MELTDOWNS

Tantrums, outbursts, and, at the extreme, aggression are a few behaviors associated with autism. Fortunately, it is possible for you to handle these behaviors and stop aggression before it gets out of hand.

Since children with autism often find communication difficult or impossible, they can become frustrated. This can lead to them acting aggressively toward people they are close to, including parents, caregivers, family, teachers, and medical staff. They can also be aggressive toward pets, or destroy toys and household items.

A meltdown is a total loss of control due to sensory overload that often results in aggression. It can begin as a tantrum and then rapidly escalate into a meltdown when the child becomes overstimulated. During a meltdown, the child becomes so disoriented that he becomes aggressive. He needs you to recognize this warning and to help rein him back in and gain control, as he is unable to do so himself.

In order to effectively stop aggression, you must first manage your own reactions before responding. If you move into aggression immediately, it will stir up your child even more. Slow yourself down, take a few deep breaths, relax your shoulders, and plant your feet firmly on the ground. This will convey to your child that you are in control of the situation and you can respond without becoming aggressive or agitated.

It is completely unacceptable for a child or adult to strike another person for any reason, at any time. This is the lesson you must convey to your child at an early age, as most people with autism do not outgrow aggression unless they are taught that it will not be tolerated.

RESPONDING TO AGGRESSION

When a child explodes, parents have to think on their feet. This isn't a problem you can analyze and try to solve, though you do need to reflect on the issue that brought the anger about for the sake of prevention. If it is aggression due to frustration, boredom, or lack of understanding, you will need to set a clear boundary with your child that aggressive behavior is not tolerated. Using strong body language where you stand up erect conveying a sense of strength in your body, using a deep and strong voice where you say no, and not babying your child are ways to set clear boundaries. This helps children understand that you are in charge.

It is often helpful to offer a communication system that the child can use to express himself. Sometimes children become aggressive because they feel like no one is listening to them. If your child effectively uses a communication system, like a keyboard to type his feelings or has picture symbols that convey his feelings, you can offer him these systems so he can nonverbally tell you what he is experiencing so you can meet his needs.

However, if a child is aggressive because of sensory overload, behavior management and a communication system will likely not have any impact. At that point, your child is in full-blown crisis and will need a powerful deep pressure technique to help him quickly calm down.

When your child is very upset or out of control, try to understand what is frustrating him by slowing yourself down and taking three breaths before making a decision on how to handle the situation.

If your child has lost control because of an inability to communicate some pressing need (he feels sick, is hungry, is frightened) his frustration will only increase if he is punished, and the tantrum will escalate. There is enough of a problem with communication without your child feeling that you are punishing him for his attempts to let you know what's on his mind. Stay firm and consistent while instructing him, either verbally if he understands or through picture systems, what is expected of him at this time.

CALMING TANTRUMS AND OUTBURSTS

It is also common for a child on the autism spectrum to display outbursts or tantrums when he feels he is not getting his way. Sometimes when a child is prevented from getting what he wants at any given moment, he may hit without warning. Parents, siblings, teachers, and caretakers are the usual targets of retaliation. For example, if your child wants a particular toy or to play with something that has been denied to him, he may scream or hit, or throw or break things. If your child then becomes distressed over the broken item, the situation will become even worse. Understand that your child is having difficulty gaining control over this repeating cycle.

In order to stop the tantrum, you need to stay firm and not give in. Outbursts can end as quickly as they begin when parents consistently set limits and make their expectations clear. To handle this situation, you can acknowledge how difficult or frustrating this is for your child and make clear what is expected of him. Let's say your child does not want to eat his dinner and wants to go straight for the dessert. You can acknowledge his frustration and give clear parameters, "I know this is hard for you and you are frustrated. First, eat dinner, then dessert." The "first, then" system gives him an idea of the order expected of him, and although he may not like it, it will redirect him to what needs to be done.

Autism and Obsessive-Compulsive Behaviors

Obsessive-compulsive disorder (OCD) is a psychiatric disorder separate from autism, although studies have shown that the two diagnoses are closely linked and may co-occur. OCD involves repetitious behaviors and thoughts that a person must perform to alleviate his anxiety. If a person diagnosed with this condition is not allowed to do these things, he can become extremely agitated.

A child with autism may have obsessive-compulsive behaviors such as:

O Lining up objects, such as trains, blocks, cars, or DVDs

O Opening or closing doors on cupboards or closets, or doors to the outside

- Spinning in circles or walking in a circle

- Stimming and hand or arm flapping

- Rocking the body back and forth

- Counting objects repeatedly for no apparent reason

- Hiding or hoarding objects

- Preoccupation with objects being placed in a chosen location

- Gestures and facial movements that resemble Tourette Syndrome

- Narrow food preference, often based on color or shape

These behaviors have two parts; the first part is the obsession with uncontrolled and unwanted thoughts. Because some people with autism may be nonverbal or have limited verbal ability, it can be difficult to know if those thoughts are present, particularly in children. The second part manifests as compulsive behaviors, which parents, teachers, and professionals can readily see.

LINES

Some experts believe that the creation of lines, and the act of lining up objects, is an attempt by a child with autism to create a sense of order to what he perceives as an out-of-control and disordered world. The sensory overload that is experienced by children with autism also makes this behavior easy to understand; lines are orderly and creating them provides a measure of control.

It is believed that individuals with autism lack the discriminatory ability to separate environmental auditory input. In other words, when the television is on, the air conditioner is running, the dog is barking, and the phone is ringing at the neighbor's house, a child with autism will perceive the sounds as all being of equal weight.

The same analogy can be applied to other senses as well. Sensory overload is a common problem for children with autism. It is easy to deduce that this "equal opportunity stimuli" would apply to visual input as well. In that case, if the visual part of the brain is on overload, lines are the perfect solution. A line is the shortest distance between two points and that makes it clean and uncluttered. Lines may not be a meaningless compulsive behavior but a way of coping with sensory overload through an order that is understandable and natural for your child.

Some parents discourage the creation of lines, resulting in frustrated and irritable children. Other parents allow the behavior, as it seems to reduce stress and anger. The negative aspect to line creation is that preoccupation and absorption may result. If that occurs, divert your child's attention to other activities such as reading a book and playing with fun sensory toys.

There are different perspectives on allowing or stopping obsessive-compulsive behaviors in children with autism. If your child is exhibiting obsessive-compulsive behaviors, early intervention can make a tremendous difference for your child's advancement, no matter your child's age. Because you are in tune with your child and his needs, don't hesitate to follow your own instincts regarding his health. A pediatric neurologist, developmental pediatrician, or child psychologist familiar with OCD and/ or autism are all resources that you should consider to determine the best forms of treatment.

The Need for Routine

Children with autism need a regular and consistent routine so they can know what to expect and when to expect it. Consistency in daily activities is very reassuring and helps to make the world feel more comfortable and manageable.

Being flexible is something that can be taught to a certain degree, but the need for routine will never disappear completely. Minimizing the shock of a change is wise, but sometimes sudden change cannot be avoided. When an unexpected event causes a change in routine and your child throws a tantrum, use the strategies previously mentioned in this chapter to understand the causes of his frustration and to calm him. Because change is inevitable, you and your child will have to adapt to new realities as the years pass. Staying in tune with his needs and anticipating problems will make day-to-day activities more successful and will help to keep the peace in your home over time.

You can create a routine for your child by setting up a predictable schedule with regular times for play, meals, therapy, school, hygiene, and bedtime. You may need to set up a routine for different days of the week if your child has different activities. The routine does not need to be the same every day; however, you do need to have an effective communication system to help her understand what will be expected on each day of the week. Sometimes the child's rigid need for routine or their reaction to a change in routine can feel very frustrating to parents. When you notice your child becoming upset, try applying your core practice by taking three deep breaths. Over time you may notice that if you can relax when your child becomes upset, she may relax and switch gears as well.

Do you notice yourself becoming aggravated by your child's need for routine? When he becomes more rigid, what do you feel or experience in your body? Can you slow yourself down and take a few breaths before you react?

Protecting Your Child from Self-Injurious Behavior

Self-injurious behavior (SIB) is another challenging facet of autism. Before you can manage this behavior properly, it is important to understand the reason behind it. If the self-injurious behavior is driven by your child's desire for attention, then ignoring the negative behavior may extinguish the negative behavior. When he has stopped, give him positive attention for appropriate behavior.

If your child is seriously hurting himself, this is not an option. You can reinforce other behavior that makes the self-injurious behavior impossible to perform (e.g., complimenting him for manipulating toys, which keeps his hands occupied). If the behavior is caused by frustration, it may be that teaching your child a way to cope or communicate will prevent the self-injury. To prevent boredom, give your child constructive options. Some SIB is so severe that it requires medication for treatment.

When your child begins to self-injure, is your first reaction to try to stop him? Can you pause, breathe, and possibly offer him an alternative? Is your first reaction to yell at him to stop him, or can you calmly, respectfully, and firmly discourage the behavior?

HEAD BANGING

Head banging is a common SIB and can have many underlying causes. It can be an indicator that the child has headaches or is feeling sick, or he is communicating that he is frustrated or feeling ignored. Because people with autism have an extremely high pain tolerance and have difficulties feeling their bodies, they do not register the effects of head banging as painful.

It is crucial to stop your child from head banging so he does not cause brain injury. In addition, it is important to determine the underlying cause of the head banging so you can prevent more of it in the future.

Techniques that may be used to relieve head banging include:

O Deep pressure to the forehead and back of the head

O Deep pressure to your child's body

O Distraction by giving him lights or toys he enjoys

O A weighted hat to give him consistent deep pressure input

Sometimes parents will put foam in areas around the bed where children may head bang during the night.

Understanding Stimming

The term "stimming" is short for self-stimulatory behavior. (It is also referred to as "stereotypic" behavior.) In a person with autism, stimming usually refers to certain behaviors, including flapping, spinning, rocking, or repetition of words and phrases.

Flapping is very common in autism, in both high- and low-functioning children. It is a rapid and repetitive hand and/or lower arm motion that resembles waving. It is linked to either strong physical actions or emotional activity, and is often one of the first symptoms that parents notice.

Researchers have suggested various reasons for why a person may engage in stereotypical behaviors. One set of theories suggests that these behaviors provide the person with sensory stimulation (i.e., the person's sense is hyposensitive). Due to some dysfunctional system in the brain or periphery, the body craves stimulation. Therefore, the person engages in these behaviors to excite or arouse the nervous system.

Another set of theories states that these behaviors are exhibited to calm a person (i.e., the person's sense is hypersensitive). That is, the environment is too stimulating and the person is in a state of sensory overload. As a result the individual engages in these behaviors to block out the over-stimulating environment, and his/her attention becomes focused inwardly.

Researchers have also shown that stereotypical behaviors interfere with attention and learning. Interestingly, these behaviors are often effective positive reinforcement if a person is allowed to engage in these behaviors after completing a task.

Flapping is not always an indication of autism. While flapping may be one of the earliest symptoms of autism, it is common for some babies to engage in this behavior. However, as a child matures, flapping should disappear. If a child at the age of eighteen months to two years continues flapping, it is something to investigate.

Some people who are not familiar with autism may feel uncomfortable around your child when he is stimming or flapping. When you see someone observing your child, do you notice that you feel ashamed of your child's habits? Notice how you feel in your body and what thoughts arise when you feel this judgment. How do you speak to your child when he is stimming in public? There is no right or wrong way to feel about your child stimming. Some parents are okay with it and will allow the child to stim, others prefer to redirect the child. If you are concerned with reducing your child's stimming, you can give him a toy or a task to do that will keep his hands and body engaged.

Your child may have involuntary habits and reactions that are caused by the sensitivity of his nervous and sensory system. These actions may be things that lessen but never completely disappear. How can your mindfulness practice help you work with yourself to accept these traits?

Professionals have different views on the treatment of flapping and stimming. The vast majority feel that if these repetitive movement patterns do not respond to the usual medications, no further treatment will be effective. Selective serotonin reuptake inhibitors (SSRIs), risperidone (Risperdal), and methylphenidate (Ritalin) are some of the medications traditionally used to treat patients with autism, but there are now many new medications in use. A good website listing these medications is *www .child-autism-parent-cafe.com/autism-medication.html.*

Preventing Elopement

Elopement means that a child escapes from home and wanders off alone. This is an especially scary behavior that may occur in children with autism. It certainly makes for sleepless nights and jittery nerves.

Before chasing a child who has escaped, try taking three breaths. This will help you calm down and think more clearly so you can make wise choices on how to handle the situation.

Sometimes the best defense is prevention. Take the time to view your house for potential escape routes to prevent elopement. Here are a few examples of what you can do:

○ Add a dead bolt on all doors that open to the outside.

○ Install a security system that monitors people entering and leaving.

○ Buy an alarm that will hang on doors to use when away from home.

○ Get a service animal (a dog is most useful for this problem).

○ Establish a routine: The child never leaves the house unsupervised.

○ Inform trusted neighbors of the possibility of elopement.

○ Notify the local police department of the possibility of elopement.

There are other things you can do to promote your peace of mind as you protect your child's safety. A large family can work in shifts so that someone always has an eye on the child with autism. If mom can't cook dinner or even escape to the bathroom for a few minutes, everyone's stress levels will rise and tempers will get shorter. The entire family must work together to lessen the stress on each family member.

If your child will wear one, an identification bracelet from MedicAlert is inexpensive and can be engraved with your child's name, address, and telephone number. Anyone calling the Medic Alert number, 1-800-625-3780, will reach a physician and specific information will be available about your child. Above the child's name have printed "Nonverbal Autistic" or "Limited Verbal Autistic" so that people are immediately aware of the child's situation.

There are various apps for the mobile phone being developed that can notify you if your child has eloped. They can accurately track his location. Suggestions for tracking can be found at: *www.iloctech.com* and *www.locationbasedgps.com/categories/Autism.*

SPECIAL CONSIDERATIONS

If you live near any potentially dangerous situations, such as water or a busy road, it is imperative that you have a locking safety system even if your child is not prone to elopement. Even just one escape could place your child in danger. Children with autism have been known to walk right in front of a moving car because they lack the ability to understand danger.

It is also wise to contact the city government for the town in which you live so that special road signs can be placed on both ends of your street to send a warning to drivers. There are signs that you can request, including a sign that says "Autistic Child."

Additionally, one of the most frightening forms of elopement can occur in the car when you are driving. Without the realization of danger, a child with autism may open a car door while the car is moving. Always have your child safety-belted and utilize child locks if available. Remove the handle on the side where your child sits. You can remove it yourself with a wrench and hammer. The cost of the repair, if you wish to have it replaced, is insignificant compared to the tragedy of a child opening the door and falling out of a moving car.

RENTAL HOUSING AND THE LAW

Laws provide for reasonable accommodation for a disabled person in rental housing. If you have a child who elopes, or escapes, it is your right to have locks installed on the inside of doorways that the child is unable to open. For younger children, consider installing slide bars placed out of reach. If you have an older child, request a keyed deadbolt. One trick that works well with a slide bar is to place it slightly out of alignment; the door handle then has to be lifted slightly, and a younger child is unable to manage this on his own.

If you live in rental housing, you may also ask your landlord to install window locks. In a pinch, a sliding window frame can have a nail hammered into it that will prevent the window from being opened any farther than desired. There are ways to jury-rig other window styles, and until a permanent fix can be implemented, don't hesitate to do what you need to do to prevent an escape.

The law provides for reasonable accommodation for disabilities. You can't demand remodeling that is frivolous, unreasonable, or abusive of the disability laws, but safety and security are reasonable expectations. Asking the landlord to fence the entire yard so your child can play outside is unreasonable, but if you live in a rental with inadequate locks or other safety concerns, the landlord must immediately address and correct these issues without penalty of eviction.

Important Points to Consider

This chapter was designed to help you understand underlying causes of challenging behaviors and how to use mindfulness to handle your reactions.

- Having empathy for your child means both offering compassion and providing firm boundaries and structure for his development.

- It is possible to distinguish between tantrums and meltdowns. During a tantrum your child will watch for your reactions and keep himself safe. During a meltdown, your child will not be aware of your reactions and can become dangerous to himself and others very rapidly.

- If you punish a child who has difficulties communicating and is losing control over an unmet need, he will escalate. Instead of reacting, stay calm yet firm while instructing him verbally or through a picture schedule what is expected of him at this time.

- If you have concerns about your child eloping and you live in rental housing, speak with your landlord to put effective safety structures into place.

 **CHAPTER 5**

Communicating with Your Child

Communication is key to many facets of life, from social to professional success to relationships and friendships. Approximately 93 percent of communication is considered nonverbal: 55 percent of communication is body language and 38 percent is the tone of voice, which leaves only 7 percent as the actual words spoken. It can feel challenging to communicate with a child who does not have verbal language, and to understand and meet her needs. However, as a parent you have the greatest connection to your child as you know your child deeply and have been "reading" her since she was a baby.

Building Communication

When parents bring home their newborn, they begin communicating nonverbally with cooing and nonsense sounds. These are the beginnings of communication. Humming tunes to a baby is another form of communication. It is through the tone and the rhythm of the voice that messages are sent. Although a baby does not have the ability to understand complex messages, she begins to learn about communication from the sounds and their cadence.

Parents learn as well how to understand nonverbal communication. They learn to recognize when their baby cries if it is a cry of hunger, discomfort, pain, or any number of things that are being communicated. Those cries, and the subsequent response by a parent, are forms of reciprocal communication.

Communicating with a nonverbal child intimidates many people. If a child understands language, even if he is unable to speak, it is hard enough to communicate, but if a child doesn't understand language, communication becomes much more difficult as well as emotionally trying. This requires the parents to be exceptionally tuned into the child, to know how to read his cues and have an effective communication system.

If only communication stayed that simple. However, as a child matures, her needs include much more than just hunger or comfort. She needs to convey emotions, complex needs, and desires, and it is very difficult to do this without language. To keep things in perspective, remember that you have already established communication with your child. Yes, it was at a very young age and, yes, it isn't a fully efficient language. But you have the basics and you know more about nonverbal communication than you realize.

TRUST YOURSELF AND PULL OUT THE STOPS

Much of the success in communication is about trust. If you believe your child will not understand, can never understand, and doesn't want to understand, you will probably find that to be true. But if you believe she can understand much more than anyone realizes and you continue to communicate with that belief, you will find that her abilities will increase.

Never assume that your words and sentences are not understood. Talk to your child slowly and calmly, and use short sentences. Don't talk down to her, and don't talk over her head. Consider your tone of voice; use gestures and every visual clue you can think of.

As the foundation begins with understanding, you will realize that more complex receptive language skills can and will develop.

Lacking Conceptual Images

People with normal speech development often communicate using concepts. Things are big or bigger, happy or joyous, under, over . . . the list is endless. The human mind is built on and works through the understanding of concepts. But for someone with autism, concepts are very difficult. How can effective communication happen without relying on the conceptual imagery everyone uses each day?

A LANGUAGE OF CONCEPT

Language by its very nature is conceptual. You probably believe, as most people do, that words are truly representative of something. If you go into an ice cream shop and ask for a large cone, you have certain expectations that you believe the other person understands. Generally, people do understand everyday concepts, and if they don't, they may ask for additional information.

Concepts within language are an obstacle for a child with autism. When a word is first learned, whether verbal or through another form of communication, the use of that word has a hard and fast rule: a dog is always a dog; a cat is always a cat. The child can't translate nonliteral uses of these words such as "hot dog" or "cat's cradle." Concepts such as "quiet," "hungry," "soft," or "tired" are hard for this child to grasp because of the severe disconnect she experiences between her body and her ability to accurately feel objects and her inability to understand variability. Using visual clues and the direct use of the objects helps her to learn how to tell time, to read, and to count money.

ECHOLALIA

As a child with autism begins to learn speech, it is common for her to repeat words without using those words for any communication or meaning. For example, a parent might show a shirt to a child and ask, "Is this your shirt or your brother's?" The response may be "Brother's." This may not mean that your child has signed off on the property in question; she may simply be repeating the last word she heard. If you are in doubt, test by using the question again, but reversing the order of words. If she repeats a different word, you can be sure it is echolalia.

When talking to your child, use universal signs to help her understand. Spread your arms to indicate "big." Mock-shiver for "cold." Use clues for your child to help her link the word with the object or action. As linkages occur, language will begin to make sense and communication will be more effective.

Echolalia is frustrating to parents because they can see that the mechanics of language, such as the voice, are working fine, yet there is no spontaneous speech. The child may repeat words she has heard during the day or words that are common to her routine. When your child engages in echolalia in response to a question, try to guide her to the correct answer and gently correct her. If she is playing alone and you hear repeated phrases and words, allow it. This may be her way of self-soothing and calming.

Receptive Language

Speech is a one-way transmission of ideas, *from* the speaker *to* the listener. Conversation would exchange ideas back and forth between two or more people. Receptive language is the ability of the human mind to hear spoken language from another person and decipher it into a meaningful mental picture or thought pattern, which is understood and then used by the recipient.

A CONFUSING WORLD

When a person has a deficit in his receptive language skills, the entire world is a mystery. People with autism are often assumed to be like people with deafness. But the inability to relate to others shows the difference between the two conditions. People with deafness can't hear sound, but they can understand the language and all the conceptual images within the words and put those to use. People with autism hear the words but don't necessarily understand the meaning behind them. They may understand a fair amount of communication in the framework of their own mental processes, or they may understand little.

Don't think your child with autism is ignoring what you say to her if she shows no reaction or withdraws into her own world. She is not deliberately tuning you out. She may not understand the meaning of what you are saying or not know how to express to you what she does understand.

IMPROVING UNDERSTANDING

A speech therapist can work with your child to improve her understanding of language. If your child is totally or essentially nonverbal, go slowly. Big picture books are helpful, as are flashcards. Avoid teaching conceptual words. If you try to explain "big" versus "small" with examples, your child may become confused. A big dog? Is the important word "dog" or "big"? Stick with nouns until your child starts to acquire receptive language skills and has a foundation to build on. Pronouns are also very difficult to understand when receptive language skills are poor. Use people's names or speak in the third person to help comprehension.

Pronouns are conceptual and should not be used unless a child has advanced speaking abilities. Speaking in the third person will be less confusing and frustrating. It is hard for a child with autism to understand that others have their own thoughts, and it's even more confusing when pronouns are used.

Expressive Speech and Sign Language

Expressive speech is the use of words and language verbally to communicate a concept or thought. Children learn their expressive speech by imitation. By hearing words from their parents, they learn how to use language as a tool. Many parents will ask, "How do I encourage my child to talk without forcing her?" Encouraging a child to speak is good, but forcing her to talk may cause great stress and is not wise. There is a fine line between the two, but after some time this interaction will become second nature. Hold up a cookie or something your child loves to eat and say "Cookie?" She will not repeat it right away, but eventually she will, if there is no hearing or other problem. When she does, give her the cookie and praise her. Some children respond well to applause; others do not like the noise. The phrase "Good job" is soon recognized as praise. The important thing is not to withhold the cookie because she doesn't say the word.

SIGN LANGUAGE

Sign language may work well because it uses gestures that are visually associated to the object they refer to and these visual associations can be easier for children with autism to understand. Children with ASD often experience difficulties in comprehending a broad range of meanings for the concepts and relations expressed through words. Sign language can help by giving the child ways to gesture more frequently and with greater complexity. This can cause a positive feedback loop as children can see that they are communicators and that the message is received and acted upon within their environment. They are also able to share experiences, which leads to a more powerful desire to communicate further. The power to be understood and to send messages that are received can create more of a desire to have more meaningful communication.

For children who have difficulties focusing or poor fine motor skills, a communication board or a tablet may be a more viable option.

Communication Boards

Many children on the autism spectrum who have limited or no verbal ability learn communication with a communication board. This is a form of augmentative and alternative communication (AAC). There are technologies such as the iPad and computer-run programs or systems as simple as a set of flashcards. Suggestions for iPad communication programs can be found at: *www.friendshipcircle.org/blog/2011/02/07/7-assistive-communication-apps-in-the-ipad-app-store*, and flashcards may be found at *www.nationalautismresources.com/autism-flash-cards.html*.

PICTURE EXCHANGE COMMUNICATION SYSTEM (PECS)

The Picture Exchange Communication System (PECS) is the most widely used communication board for children and adults with autism. The beauty of this tool is that the learning curve is very low; the system is easy to figure out and can be used immediately.

For children with ASD, visual strategies and supports (i.e., pictures, photographs, objects, words) increase their understanding of what is being said and what is expected of them.

The following are acronyms commonly used when discussing picture symbol communication systems for children with autism.

PCS stands for Picture Communication Symbols, which are the symbols in the Boardmaker software program. ("PCS" is sometimes mistakenly interpreted as "PECS"). *Boardmaker* is the software program containing thousands of pictures that can be used to create picture schedules, manual communication boards, device overlays, etc. Find out more information and get downloadable symbols and instructions at *www.mayer-johnson.com.*

PECS is a communication program designed to develop functional communication skills in students. PECS is designed for students who are not initiating communication or approaching their communication partners. It teaches children communication in multiple stages. In the early phase, students are taught how to request highly desired items by delivering a single picture symbol to the hand of a communication partner. In the later phases, the students combine symbols on a sentence strip to exchange with a communication partner to make requests or comments.

To find out more about this system, check out the website at *www.pecs .com.*

BUILDING A COMMUNICATION BOARD

If you choose to use a communication board, you can test it out very easily with your child. Take photographs, or cut pictures out of magazines, and have them laminated. Home laminating machines can also be purchased and will be handy to have around. Laminate about ten to fifteen cards, each one just a few inches square. Attach the cards together with a loose-leaf ring—these rings can be purchased separately—and show them to your child. As she learns that pointing to the picture of the television communicates that she wishes to watch a program, the value of the cards will be learned. Make them relevant to your child's life so they are uniquely her own. Put them in a fanny pack and have her wear it so she has constant access to the cards.

Other Communication Methods

One method of communication that is very reliable for individuals with autism is the keyboard. Many children who cannot speak are extremely efficient readers and writers. They may not be able to say they are thirsty and need a drink of water, but they are able to type it on a simple word-processing program. Even a simple text file on a desktop computer, a laptop, or handheld computer device will work.

If your child seems to understand language and reads, try typing a simple question to them. "What is your name?" to start. She may look at you, unsure of what you want. Say the question while you point to the words on the screen and then point to the keyboard. If she understands how to communicate through writing, she will attempt to provide the answer. Coach her a bit as you begin. You will know very quickly whether this tool works for your child.

If you elect to use keyboard communication, consider a handheld computer device or an iPad to help your child. It is also possible to play games on a handheld device, which can be a great deal of fun and a good distraction for times when a child might be bored.

In addition, a wise teacher or speech therapist will know that there are many nonverbal methods of communication and will work hard to find whatever it takes to establish effective communication. However, if you feel the system being taught to your child is not the best one for her, talk with your child's teachers or request a consultation with an assistive technology consultant. This may have to be done by requesting a new IEP (Individualized Education Program) (discussed in Chapter 12). Don't be afraid to challenge a system that doesn't seem to be working or is causing your child stress.

Another communication tool is the method of facilitated communication (FC). This technique involves another person assisting a nonverbal person's efforts to communicate. The support may be as simple as providing encouragement to boost the self-confidence of someone who is unable to speak. It can also involve steadying or guiding a hand to pictures or words if necessary. People with tremors, nerve damage, or poor muscle control may require some physical assistance.

The most important thing any parent, caretaker, family member, teacher, or professional can remember about communication is that there is no one right way that works for every child. A child with autism is just like any other child: each is unique and will respond to different styles of learning and working. If one child works well with keyboard communication and another can't figure it out but is a whiz with PECS, it doesn't mean one child is more advanced than the other. It simply means that they have two different methods of communicating.

Important Points to Consider

Much of your success in communication with your child is based on trust. When your child realizes that you want to understand her and you believe in her, you may be surprised over time at how she shares her wants and needs with you!

O If you believe that your child cannot understand you, you will have a difficult time figuring out how to communicate with her.

O If you believe that she can understand much more than anyone realizes and you continue to communicate with that belief, her communication skills will increase.

O Communicate with your child slowly and calmly, and use short sentences. Don't talk down to her, and don't talk over her head.

O Commonly used communication systems are communication boards, PECS, sign language, and keyboarding.

 **CHAPTER 6**

Practical Approaches to Handling Tantrums, Meltdowns, and Discipline

Children with autism, like all children, require a balance of fun and enjoyment, and firm guidance. Discipline does not need to be an angry or negative experience. If handled according to conscious parenting principles, it can be positive and motivating for everyone. Remember that positive reinforcement is much more effective than negative, and that applying mindfulness tools before disciplining your child will give you a chance to evaluate your emotions before you react. This will make sure you are as centered as possible.

Temper Tantrums versus Meltdowns

Life with a child who frequently tantrums or has meltdowns is extremely challenging and downright exhausting. Many parents have a very difficult time deciphering if the child's behavior is a tantrum or a meltdown and how to handle it. The following information will give you a preliminary understanding of the differences and how you can manage these different reactions.

TEMPER TANTRUMS

A temper tantrum is usually straightforward. A child does not get his own way and, as grandma would say, "pitches a fit." Tantrums have several qualities that distinguish them from meltdowns, including:

- A child having a tantrum will look occasionally to see if his behavior is getting a reaction.

- A child in the middle of a tantrum will take precautions to be sure he won't get hurt.

- A child who throws a tantrum will attempt to use the social situation to his benefit.

- When the situation is resolved, the tantrum will end as suddenly as it began.

- A tantrum will give you the feeling that the child is in control, although he would like you to think he is not.

- A tantrum is thrown to achieve a specific goal; once the goal is met, things return to normal.

- Tantrums usually result when a child makes a request to have or do something that the parent denies. Upon hearing the parent's "no," the child uses the tantrum as a last-ditch effort to get his way.

If you feel that you are being manipulated by a tantrum, you are right. A tantrum is nothing more than a power play by a person not mature enough to play a subtle game of internal politics. Hold your ground and remember who is in charge.

Handling Tantrums

A temper tantrum from a child with autism does *not* de-escalate when you ignore him. Firm, consistent rules and boundaries have to be given repeatedly, as these children have a very difficult time remembering and generalizing instructions.

In addition, parents must be in agreement on what behaviors are to be disciplined and what is to be overlooked. Each parent shares in both parenting and disciplining. Parents must be in agreement about how they feel about discipline. If a child throws a tantrum and these decisions have not been made, it will be difficult to know how to handle it. The middle of your child's meltdown or tantrum is not the best time to discuss child-rearing philosophies.

You have to learn that you are in control, not the child. This is not a popularity contest. You are not there to wait on your child and indulge his every whim. Simply because he screams and demands something does not mean that giving it will serve his best interests. Once he realizes he is not going to get his way, he will begin to calm down. During a tantrum, children with autism will screech so loudly that if someone did not know better, they would think the child was being tortured. They are so headstrong, but you can do it—be strong, dig in your heels, and let them roar!

When it comes to handling a tantrum in public, try these tips:

O Recognize the signs of an impending tantrum: screeching, stomping, or hitting.

O Determine if there is a certain trigger and what it is.

- If the trigger is fairly insignificant, such as your child wanting to hold a red ball in the store, decide whether it is worth it. A red ball is a small price to pay for a quiet shopping trip.

- If the trigger is something that is not possible to resolve (such as the one in the tractor story later in this chapter), try to distract your child by moving to another location and finding a substitute to divert his attention.

- If you are in a restaurant, reach for a new or very special toy he will enjoy that you have hidden in your purse.

- As you are working to distract your child, speak firmly and calmly to him about his behavior and let him know that it needs to stop. Don't dwell on what he can't have at that moment, but reiterate that he needs to slow down. Stay calm so that he has no idea you are panicking over the thought that he might lose it.

Remember, right in the middle of a wedding may not be the best time to try to work with behavior modification. It would be best not to take a child prone to severe tantrums or meltdowns to a special occasion such as a wedding. Other people do have the right to an undisturbed environment. However, in the real world, the everyday world, your child has to learn to operate in society, and society will hopefully learn to deal with children who have autism. However, it is more prudent to leave an area if others are being disturbed unfairly or if you feel the situation could become dangerous.

Managing Meltdowns with Conscious Parenting

The meltdown is a loss of control due to sensory overload. It can begin as a tantrum and then rapidly escalate into a meltdown when the child becomes overstimulated. The child needs you to recognize this and rein him back in, as he is unable to do so, desperately needing your help to regain control. Meltdowns can leave parents at their wit's end, unsure of what to do, as meltdowns can be very loud, frustrating, potentially dangerous, and exhausting.

QUALITIES OF MELTDOWNS

The following is a list of common meltdown qualities you may see with your child:

○ The child with autism does not notice or care whether those around him are reacting to his behavior.

○ A child in the middle of a meltdown does not consider his own safety.

○ A child in a meltdown has no interest or involvement in what's happening around him.

○ Meltdowns will usually continue as though they are moving under their own power and wind down slowly unless the child or his caregiver knows how to take him out of sensory overload.

○ A meltdown conveys the feeling that no one is in control.

Health issues such as migraines can also cause meltdowns. A child who suffers from migraines may be at greater risk for a meltdown because the migraine acts as a trigger. A migraine may come on suddenly and the pain is so debilitating, a child's behavior may spiral quickly downward, resulting in a meltdown. Watch for telltale signs such as sensitivity to light, head holding, or unusual sensitivity to sound.

HOW TO HANDLE MELTDOWNS

If your child launches into a meltdown, remove him from an area where he could be injured or where he might cause damage. Many children benefit from a deep pressure system that helps them calm and reorganize their senses. The following is a list to help you spot when a tantrum is turning into a meltdown:

- O The child will stop looking at you and checking for your reaction.

- O He cannot focus his eyes on any human being or fixed object. His eyes appear to be "rolling around in their sockets."

- O He will get a subtle look of panic at first. If the meltdown escalates, he will look totally panicked.

- O His body movements become extremely jerky and erratic.

- O His breath is shallow and caught up in the upper chest. There is no diaphragmatic breathing. This is called "emotional breathing."

TO MARKET, TO MARKET

Inevitably, your child will experience a meltdown in a large, brightly lit discount store. Every parent knows about these stores—the one-stop shopping that turns into an ordeal and fiasco. A parent related the following story about her son, and any parent of a child with autism will laugh and cry at the same time; they all know what this is like.

> *"We went in for groceries and various items. It was a big shopping trip and I couldn't find a babysitter that day. I also couldn't put it off any longer. We did okay until we went by the home gardening section. A big, and I mean very big, lawn sprinkler was on display—a sprinkler that was a dead ringer for the tractor that my little boy loves, all bright green and yellow and just about the right size for him to sit on. At first he quietly asked 'tractor,' or, should I say, demanded it. I could see the look. I knew he had decided the 'tractor' was coming home with us. And I knew it wasn't. The volume of his voice went higher and higher until you could hear the word* tractor *being screeched all over the store! We made our way to the checkout line, but by then, he was in complete meltdown. I am sure everyone thought I was the meanest mom in the world for not buying my little boy a toy tractor. The meltdown continued into the parking lot and into the car; he was sweating, crying,*

screaming, and attempting to hit anything or anyone he could. He totally lost it. I was exhausted and so was he." She added, "I now make an extra effort to find a babysitter and have my radar up to scope out the aisles around us to avoid any more tractors."

This mom handled a difficult situation well. She had shopping that had to be done; this wasn't an optional trip to the store. And once the meltdown was in full swing, she was almost done. It wouldn't have been convenient for her to leave the store and return later to redo an enormous amount of shopping. She kept her cool, didn't give in, and didn't worry about the opinions of others while her son spun totally out of control.

If your child begins a meltdown by putting his hands over his ears or eyes, you can be sure he is experiencing sensory overload. The best thing to do is remove him from the overstimulating area and provide deep pressure to calm him.

HOW OTHERS RESPOND

The little boy with, or in this case without, the tractor had a real advantage that day. His mother was not threatened or concerned about the opinions of others. It has been said that parents of kids with special needs have to develop thicker skins, and it must be true. But regardless of how thick-skinned you are, an insult to your child cuts, and cuts deeply.

For some reason, in public places many people feel it is their duty to point out all of the mistakes they believe you are making in raising your child. This is even more common if your child is mentally challenged or if the child "expert" has no children. Just remember: You can't change the world; you can only change your little corner of it. How your child feels and how you affect his life are far more important.

It is very common for people in public places such as the store in the tractor incident to stare and make comments very critical of a child in the middle of a meltdown. People will say things about your lack of control over your child or direct unflattering comments toward your child, and as much as you would like to throttle them or talk back, resist the urge. Excuse your child's behavior politely with the brief explanation of "He has autism" and drop it. If a person persists in making comments and it is clear she is not interested in educating herself, move yourself and your child to another location. If, on the other hand, it is a staff member who is making snide comments at the place you are visiting, ask to speak with a manager. The supervisor needs to know that the staff member does not understand the problems of a child with a disability and steps should be taken to educate the individual.

When Your Child Does Not Understand

A child who does not understand what type of behavior is wanted or expected is more challenging to deal with when a tantrum occurs. It is important to remain calm. If your child is already on the defensive and you are upset, you will aggravate the situation. Keep your voice even, quiet, and calm no matter what happens.

The primary tool a parent has with a child in a tantrum is a distraction. It is useless to try to reason with a child who does not understand that his actions are not acceptable. Molding a child's behavior through distraction and positive reinforcement will be a much more effective tool and will hopefully prevent future tantrums.

Distraction is 50 percent preparation and 50 percent creativity. Preparation is the easy part. Mom or Dad can put items to distract their child in a backpack or tote bag to have when a tantrum begins. Being able to pull "the rabbit out of the hat" is your best bet. Comforting toys, such as a favorite stuffed animal, are wise choices, as are toys that are so fascinating they just can't be ignored.

Will I know if the distraction has things under control? Your child will either continue his tantrum or become engrossed in the distraction toy and the tantrum will fade. If your child throws the "distraction" toy back at you, it is a sign you need to give him another option.

Think of toys your child enjoys and finds pleasure in. Every child is different; there is no "stop-the-tantrum-toy" available. Use the knowledge you have of your child and let his reactions guide you as you consider helpful distractions.

Behavior Modification

Which is easier: handling a tantrum or giving in? You may feel right now that you have little control over your child's tantrums and meltdowns, but there are methods you can learn to minimize the frequency and severity of the outbursts.

Working with a child's behavior is always the first step a parent should take. If you can modify his undesirable behavior, your child ultimately will be happier and those around him will be as well. Don't ever think you are being cruel by working to alter unacceptable behaviors. That is your job as a parent. You will be met with resistance; no one likes to change, least of all a child with autism. But at times, change is necessary, and when a child is prone to tantrums, he must learn new behaviors.

APPLIED BEHAVIOR ANALYSIS (ABA)

Applied behavior analysis (ABA) is one of the most widely used methods of treating children with autism. The goal in working with children with autism has been to modify behaviors that are inappropriate and replace them with appropriate behaviors. The popular and effective Lovaas Institute approach to ABA can be reviewed on their website, *www.lovaas .com.*

By a twist of fate, Dr. Lovaas began working with children with autism and observed that modifying behaviors was not that difficult. The hard part was keeping those behaviors solidly in place after the behavior had been successfully changed.

Dr. Lovaas realized that the main difference in behaviors between children with autism and those without could be found in their learning styles. Children who do not have autism are constantly learning. However, a child with autism goes to school and learns for a prescribed number of hours each day. When he returns home, the structured learning is over for the day and he retreats into his own world. Parents were then taught how to continue the ABA therapy at home and changes in their child's behaviors became permanent.

A newer style of ABA is called applied verbal behavior or VB. It uses B.F. Skinner's 1957 analysis of verbal behavior to teach and reinforce speech, along with other skills. A verbal behavioral program will focus on getting a child to realize that language will get him what he wants, when he wants it. Requesting is often one of the first verbal skills taught; children are taught to use language to communicate, rather than just to label items. Learning how to make requests also should improve behavior. Some parents report that verbal behavior seems like a more natural form of ABA.

NEUROFEEDBACK THERAPY (NFT)

The idea behind neurofeedback therapy (NFT) is that patients can be taught how to change their brain waves, which could then help to control focus, anxiety, mood, and behavior. A recent scientific study suggests that improvement in the condition of children with autism after undergoing NFT occurs because it addresses a co-morbid condition of attention deficit disorder (ADD). A child undergoing neurofeedback has a special wire or electrode placed on his scalp as well as one on each ear. He is placed in front of a computer, and a video-like game displays his brain waves. A therapist then shows parent and child how the child's thought patterns can change the brain waves. The child receives points when his brain waves are altered in certain ways. Initially, the therapist will want to see the child several times a week, but then the sessions revert to just once a week. This is a major time commitment for a parent and child.

Medications

When the behavior of a child with autism becomes unpredictable, it is miserable for him as well as everyone around him. Children with autism can lash out physically, kicking, hitting, and/or biting, when they become angry. Some children's aggression can be handled through behavioral management techniques, while other children's aggression can be so severe that they require medication.

There are several medications used to help in the control of unpredictable behaviors that children with autism will display. Parents are often reluctant to use medication, but there are times when it is appropriate and necessary. It is vital to remember that an out-of-control child is not a happy child, but a child who needs help. You have not failed as a parent if you and your physician decide medications are appropriate for your child.

One medication used for aggression is risperidone (Risperdal). This is currently approved only for patients over age eighteen. If your teenager is on this medication, watch for excessive weight gain and facial tics. If either of these occurs, visit your teen's physician to decide if the dosage needs to be adjusted. Clonidine is another medication commonly prescribed to reduce anxiety.

If medications are prescribed for your child and you are concerned about side effects or long-term use, talk to a pharmacist about your concerns. A pharmacist is one of the best resources for a discussion of these issues as well as for advice on medications, interactions between medicines, and which over-the-counter medications are safe for your child to use. In a support group meeting, ask other parents what medications they have used and how they feel about them; a support group can be very helpful as a medication becomes part of the routine. However, remember that these medicines are very potent, so if you have serious concerns or questions, it would be wise to seek professional advice.

Important Points to Consider

In order for children with autism to feel comfortable and safe, they require a balance of activities they enjoy and consistent guidance from their parents.

O Discipline can be firm but does not have to be an angry or negative experience.

- You are not being cruel when you stop unacceptable behaviors. That is your job as a parent. Expect to be met with resistance, as all children, whether they have autism or not, will test their parents to get their own way.

- Many children can be distracted during a tantrum using an object or activity that they enjoy.

- Some children's aggression can be modified through behavior management techniques, while other children's aggression can be so severe and dangerous that they require medication.

 **CHAPTER 7**

Autism and Your Marriage

Having a child with autism can be hard on a marriage and a family. It may seem difficult for a couple, particularly when they are young, to remain a couple when they have a child who is so far from what they had anticipated. So many professionals become a part of your life that you may feel they have become part of your marriage. Remembering that you are still the same two people who fell in love, married, and planned to live happily together may seem like remembering a distant dream. Marriages that do succeed are ones where both partners work on keeping their connection, love, and relationship alive.

How Mom Is Affected

Pregnancy is an exciting time for a woman. The growing infant within her—as it begins to move and kick and then show a silhouette on an ultrasound—is the person she most anticipates meeting. It doesn't matter if it is a first child or the second or the tenth. This baby is often the focus of her thoughts.

When the baby is born and the doctor announces whether it is a boy or girl, invariably the first question heard is "Is everything all right?" And what a relief it is when all ten fingers and toes are present and there are no disabilities. A healthy child has come into the world.

A CHILD REGRESSING

It is a shock to parents when they see their child's developmental progress begin to slip away slowly. Their beautiful baby, now approaching the toddler stage, with her few words and joyful reactions to the world around her, is changing. The words are fewer and fewer until they are heard no more. The interactive baby, who chuckled and had sparkling eyes just looking at Mom and Dad, now seems enclosed in a world of darkness where no one else can go.

Their child will no longer look at them, no longer tries to learn new words or even use those already learned, and doesn't seem to hear them. They will likely ask each other: "What have we done wrong?"

THE FIVE STAGES

There are five stages that a person progresses through from infancy to adulthood. Although the stages are the same for children with and without autism, what occurs when a child has autism is different than what happens with a child who is not autistic.

O **Infancy**—Hopes, dreams, and visions of a new life are shattered with the realization that something has gone wrong.

O **Toddler years**—The child's mother begins to realize that the problems are not going away and must be coped with.

○ **Young school age**—More dreams are lost as a child enters school and Mom can see the contrast between her child and other children.

○ **Older school age**—The child makes progress, but new concerns develop over challenges brought by puberty, adolescence, and the beginning of young adulthood.

○ **Adulthood**—As the child becomes an adult, Mom and Dad become aware that they, too, are aging and they begin to worry what will happen to their child when they are no longer able to provide care.

This is a lot for young parents to absorb. And parents often think about all five stages within a few months of the diagnosis. Stress, fear, denial, anxiety, confusion, anger, depression, and sadness are inevitable. It may be one of the hardest times in their lives.

DIAGNOSIS AND ADJUSTMENT

Mothers are deeply affected when professionals begin the process of diagnosing their child. The protective and maternal instincts within a mother are natural, so she is likely to resent all the "experts" who have suddenly intruded into the middle of her family's life.

Mothers may feel frustrated when the experts can't give an immediate diagnosis. The testing for autism and other related conditions can take quite some time, and frustration with medical and other professionals is normal. The acceptance of or adjustment to the diagnosis that will eventually come is at this point a long time off, and it is a tumultuous time.

Eventually all of the emotions that run amok within the mother will settle down, and although none of them ever disappears entirely, they generally become more manageable and acceptance occurs. Ideally, Mom will begin to adjust to the situation and start to reset goals and plans, accommodating the child's needs and abilities within that framework. There will always be times when she will feel sad or depressed; she will have spikes of anger at the situation when a problem arises that isn't easily solved, but she will have learned to accept or adjust and do what moms do best: love her child.

How Dad Is Affected

Dads are also affected by the realization that their child has been diagnosed on the autism spectrum, but the reactions of a father can be different from those of a mother. Men usually want to fix the problem quickly; when they learn they can't, they must reach an understanding that they have not failed. It is not their fault the child has autism any more than it is the mother's fault. Just like mothers, fathers progress through stages of understanding as their child with autism goes through life stages:

- **Infancy**—When a dad has a new infant, his pride and delight are unparalleled. When something goes wrong, it is hard for many fathers to come to terms with the disability, and they may take a long time to accept it. Usually a father grapples with acceptance of his child's autism longer than a mother.

- **Toddler years**—Realization begins to force its way into a father's mind. Fathers will either react with acceptance of the situation and begin to find ways to cope with it, or deny that it exists or look to blame someone. Denial is a common reaction for men, as well as many women, because they feel responsible for the events that occur within their family.

- **Young school age**—As a child enters school, fathers begin to see the deficits and often have trouble seeing the child's progress. It is important that therapists, physicians, and the child's mother point out the progress being made so that the father can see the glass as half full. This stage is normal, and it will pass. Many dads feel responsible and frustrated that they can't fix the problem.

○ **Older school age**—This is a time where fathers really shine if they have come to acceptance, which many have by this stage. The progress is evident and now the issues are ones that men can handle more comfortably. They must meet specific challenges and problem solving is a needed skill. Dad may find his problem-solving skills to be very useful and he will feel less like a failure and more like a dad.

○ **Adulthood**—Like Mom, Dad becomes aware that his child has become an adult and that he will not always be there to protect her. By this time, hopefully he and Mom will have started estate and financial planning to protect their child, and worked on solving the issues that will face her after they are gone.

LEARNING TO COPE

Dad has a lot to absorb, just as Mom does. Men have different coping mechanisms than women, so they will process and absorb all of this differently. It is important for Mom to remember that Dad's method of dealing with the diagnosis of their child is no less valid than her own. If it seems that a father isn't handling the situation well, perhaps there is some denial involved, but given time the acceptance or adjustment to the diagnosis will most likely occur.

A strong family is the key to coping with a child who has autism. For a father, it is vital that he maintains strong bonds with his spouse and all of his children. It helps to keep the family strong when the father can provide needed physical, emotional, and spiritual leadership, so his wife or partner and other family members do not carry too great a burden.

It is hard for parents to adapt to the loss of the dreams they had for their child, and there will be a period of adjustment as Mom and Dad establish new goals. Women can do a lot to help their husbands adjust by understanding the psychology of wanting to "make it okay" that is often inherent in a male's nature.

Eventually, both parents will accept or adjust, and establish a routine. As these processes are happening, both Mom and Dad may have difficulties remembering that their marriage is the first priority. Taking care of each other will enable them to take care of the rest of their family, and that includes their child with autism.

Keeping ASD from Affecting Your Marriage

The strongest piece of advice most therapists will give a couple that has a child with autism is: "Do not allow autism to become your entire life." It is so easy to eat, breathe, and sleep autism. When this happens, it can result in short tempers, communication difficulties, allowing your life as a couple to fade away, and the worst possible situation, turning to others rather than each other for companionship and support.

If you allow autism to take over your life, you will become socially isolated. When you can learn to turn to each other for support and go to events, support groups, and other activities as a couple, this can strengthen your bond. You can become stronger because of autism and not allow it to unravel your marriage. It just takes time, effort, and a lot of love.

MAINTAINING AND CREATING INTIMACY

One of the most difficult things in a marriage, let alone a marriage with a child with special needs, is maintaining the intimacy unique to marriage. When a couple goes from being a man and a woman to being a mom and a dad, they often find it hard to remember they are still a man and a woman! The special intimacy that you knew before you had a child is just as important as it was before, perhaps even more so.

Here are some suggestions if you feel that your relationship is struggling and autism is running your life.

○ Attend counseling, both individually and as a couple. Counseling can help the woman receive support, so she does not feel she is handling everything by herself. Counseling can help the man understand what the woman is going through, to learn that handling the children and the household is a team effort and is not only the responsibility of the woman. Counseling can help you learn to work as a team. Sometimes the woman is not allowing the husband to help, and the counselor can assist with opening up the lines of communication so roles are balanced.

○ Create a shared list and a schedule of responsibilities. Consider dividing the responsibilities to relieve overload. For instance, the mother may be in charge of medical needs and doctor appointments while the husband is in charge of therapies and schoolwork. If scheduling difficulties come up, talk about how you can trade or share a responsibility.

○ Use your mindfulness practices to help you when you talk. There will be times when you need to air your feelings and talk about how you want to handle challenges, and it is most effective if you can communicate in kind, supportive, respectful ways.

○ Spend some time apart. So much of the relationship is spent focusing on the children, particularly the child with autism. Give each other the opportunity to get away from the household for a while. This is healthy for everyone, including the children.

○ Communicate in a straightforward way so the man can understand when the woman is getting worn out. Do not wait for her to ask for your help; offer to step in and help. It is then the woman's role to allow his help.

○ Once you have gotten it together as a team, invite family or friends who want to help. Show them what they can do to assist so that you can have the freedom to go out as a couple to dinner, to the movies, or simply for a walk. If transition to bedtime is difficult, some parents will put their child to bed first and then have the babysitter come over.

○ The maternal, protective bond is very powerful. It can be very challenging for mothers to leave their child with someone else; however, this can cause more harm to the child than help her. By not allowing help, the mother loses her freedom and becomes stuck. Generally, children with autism are most aggressive with their mothers because their mothers are in their face all the time. Having other people care for your child gives *everyone* a healthy break.

Your Priorities

It is important to keep your priorities in order. Doing so will help you feel more relaxed and calm. When people have their priorities out of order or think everything in life is a priority, they are highly stressed and have difficulty focusing and enjoying life. Most parents tend to put their children first, their mate second, and themselves last. Consider taking care of yourself first, then taking care of your mate, which will allow you to more effectively take care of and enjoy your children.

TAKING CARE OF YOURSELF IS FIRST PRIORITY

You can't take care of anyone else unless you take care of yourself first. If you've ever flown, you've heard the flight attendant say "In the event of a change in cabin pressure, panels above your head will open revealing oxygen masks . . . Remember to secure your own mask before assisting others." You have to attend to yourself first in order to be physically, emotionally, mentally, and spiritually available to your mate and children.

MAKING YOUR MATE A PRIORITY

One of the most important priorities in your life is your spouse. People, especially mothers, tend to let this priority slip and put their children above their marriage. Although it sounds noble not to put anything above your children, in reality it is harmful for everyone, including the children. The marriage is the foundation of the family, not the children.

Many people would feel guilty putting another adult, even a spouse, above their children. It is not a matter of viewing one person as more

> One of the best things you can do for yourself, for your marriage, and for your children is to take a few minutes each day to have some quiet time and do your core practice. It will rebalance and refresh your spirit and help make things easier to manage.

important than another. It is an understanding of how we can most effectively handle our obligations and responsibilities. A child cannot feel secure and grow up to the best of her ability if the family's foundation is unstable.

If a child's parents love each other and work hard to create the best relationship they possibly can, their child will feel this security. It has been said that there is no greater gift a father can give his children than to love their mother. It is also true that a mother can show nothing greater to her children than love for their father.

CHILDREN AS A PRIORITY

Most parents have no difficulty with this one! Children quickly, almost automatically, become the lights of our lives. Children can be a gift and bring joy, happiness, frustration, irritation, laughter, tears, and every possible emotion into our lives.

Some parents can find it hard to remember that their children are more important than their work. Careers are a lifelong project, and a person with an occupation doesn't always understand that a child's needs are more critical than a deadline at the office. It is so easy to be caught up in the mentality that "it has to be done right now." In reality, the only jobs that have to be done "right now" are those of trauma surgeons and the like. So, if you are a physician, paramedic, firefighter, or have a career where peoples' lives are on the line, you may have to make some extra efforts to keep your job in its proper perspective without ignoring the needs of family members who depend on you.

For the majority of people, most career obligations can fit into a normal workday. There should be only a few career-related urgencies that will keep you from your child's soccer games, concerts, or other activities that are part of the growing-up process. There will be many activities that your child with autism can participate in, and it is important for you to be there if possible.

Yes, there will be times you can't attend an activity or be at a doctor's appointment without risking your job, and in those situations all you can do is your best. Ask yourself if what you are doing at work is truly something you can't leave or if it is a self-imposed deadline. If it is something you are putting on yourself, take some time to analyze your priorities.

Valuing Extended Family

If you're like most people, you are part of a larger family unit; there are grandparents, in-laws, cousins, and other people who are part of your life. Those family members are important to you, your spouse, and your child. Growing up within an extended family is a wonderful privilege and provides another layer to a secure foundation for children. Extended family can be there to help you, just as you help them, and be part of very special relationships and memories.

However, it is important not to let the extended family relationships take over your life. This is where your priority system comes into play. In any family, there are social occasions to attend: parties, showers, weddings, and other celebrations are part of the family experience. Most of these are good for the family and good for children, but they don't need to dictate your family's schedule. Pacing your family's schedule is important. If your child is easily overstimulated by too much activity, choose family occasions that are the least stressful for her. If you are involved in social activities two or three times a week, you and your child may become too exhausted to attend to basic family needs. Saying "no" occasionally to various get-togethers is sometimes the best decision. Explain the situation to your extended family so they can still be involved with your child and learn as much about autism as possible.

Handling Your Work

If you already have a career established when you learn that your child has autism, it would be wise to schedule a meeting with your immediate supervisor and explain the situation. You can share the FAQ in the appendix of this book to help him understand autism. Having your supervisor's understanding about the various challenges will help prevent misunderstandings in the future should you require time away from work due to your child's various doctor, therapy, or school appointments.

When you explain to your employer that your child has autism, emphasize that you will do your best to not allow this to affect your work performance. Keep in mind that your employer is there to run an efficient business. Volunteer to make up any missed time if this is a possibility.

If you work for a large company, you may find that your company would be willing to become involved with autism awareness causes. Many companies will rally behind an employee who has a child on the autism spectrum and donate money to various fundraising campaigns.

Friends, Hobbies, and Everything Else

Life can seem overwhelming at times, particularly when you have just learned that your child has autism. You may think that, because autism is now part of your life, you will no longer be able to enjoy all of the people and interests you have had over the years. Use your mindfulness practices when you find yourself becoming overwhelmed to help you reflect on where there is meaning in your life.

Friends are a link to sanity. Meeting with them on a regular basis will help you maintain your mental health. They remind you that there is a world out there, and conversations beyond how to take care of children are a welcome escape. Be careful, though, that you don't rely on friends more than a spouse, or spend so much time with friends that other parts of your life are neglected. Visit with friends and make plans to do things that have nothing to do with autism, but keep those relationships in their proper perspective.

Hobbies, sports, and activities of any kind promote health and well-being, both mentally and physically. If you enjoyed certain hobbies or travel before, try to continue these pursuits, at least on a limited basis. Yes, you will have to make adjustments, but as long as you keep things in the proper perspective, you should be able to do many of the things that are important to you and your family.

As mentioned earlier, it is not unusual to find parents spending hours each day on the Internet, in libraries, in public records, or private book collections to find the one thing that may "fix" their child's autism. It is important that parents recognize their vulnerability in this area. A tantalizing product that may cure your child is hard to resist. Keep in mind that you need to have a balance of meeting all of your family members' needs, as well as discernment to be able to determine if what you are being offered is viable and ethical.

Important Points to Consider

Having a child with autism can be hard on a marriage and a family. Marriages that do succeed are ones where both partners work on keeping their connection, love, and relationship alive.

- If you find that autism has become your entire life, consider using your mindfulness practices, or go to counseling or a support group, to help you deal with your concerns and get a new perspective.

- Priorities are yourself first, then your mate, and then your children. If you put your children first over yourself and your mate, you will get burned out and your relationship will suffer.

- The maternal bond is very powerful. A mother can find it very challenging to leave her child with family or a friend; however, not doing so may limit the child's social growth.

- Explore activities that will help you feel better, both mentally and physically, such as hobbies, sports, or visiting with a friend. Doing so will positively contribute to your marriage and family life.

CHAPTER 8

Conscious Parenting As a Single Parent

Parenting is full of challenges, and while single parenting can be stressful, it can also be very fulfilling. The real trick to success as a parent, whether single or married, is to not lose yourself in the parenting process. It takes a little more effort, organization, and of course, a lot of love to be a single parent. There are some special circumstances to consider when you are the single parent of a child with autism. While at times it might be difficult handling everything by yourself, with the proper tools and mindset you can minimize the struggles and maximize your successes.

Unique Challenges

Being a single parent can be an exhausting but incredibly rewarding job. However, there are some issues that every single parent needs to be aware of, including:

- O Single parenting will require you to establish a lot of structure so that your household will run smoothly.

- O You may need to regularly utilize your mindfulness practices, and/ or go to counseling, so that you do not get lost in feeling sorry for your child or yourself.

THE DIFFICULTY OF A SOCIAL LIFE

Everyone needs social interaction, and a single parent of a child with autism is no exception. In addition to caring for your child, you may be working full time, meeting the needs of your other children, and taking care of the home—leaving you with little free time.

It is important to carve out time in your schedule for social activities. These can be whatever activities you enjoy that bring you some balance and happiness. Having a social life will help calm your emotions by giving you other things to think about besides your child's needs. Having a life beyond your child will help him grow, as he will be exposed to other people who can play with him and teach him new skills.

IMPACT OF ISOLATING

Sometime a single parent will isolate and become overly focused on his or her child. This will make the child too dependent on his parent. Children with autism already have difficulties developing relationships with others. Such dependence can prevent an already rigid child from learning how to develop flexibility or how to adapt to alternative ways of doing things. It is very normal for parents to be concerned about their children; however, they can become too overprotective and not let the child out of their sight. This creates a cycle of feeling trapped, and can lead to feelings of depression and to not taking care of themselves.

NO PARTNER TO COMMISERATE WITH DAILY

One major advantage that married parents have is companionship. Yes, there are many other advantages as well, but nothing is quite like being with a person who knows and understands your daily schedule. Having someone with whom you can pour out your frustrations and successes of the day is a relief. A local support group that includes single parents might be helpful. Some support groups have a network of parents who are on "phone duty" that you can call at any time when you need to talk or vent your emotions.

DEALING WITH YOUR EX

Children with autism may seem to be unaware of the environment around them, but they are much more in tune with the emotions of others than it appears. If the adults are arguing or fighting, the child will feel this and can act out. By keeping their own tempers, the adults in the situation can prevent this. Remember that although your relationship may be over, the relationship both of you have with your child is not.

A MULTITUDE OF CHALLENGES

Every single parent with a child with ASD will find challenges and obstacles. Some of these challenges will require solutions unique to the individual family. Issues that can arise include:

○ Preventing elopement or escape when the parent is temporarily unavailable

○ Having safety measures in place to prevent accidents

○ Protecting younger children from an older sibling with ASD

○ If you have a four-door car, making sure that the back doors cannot be opened while the car is moving

○ Budgeting carefully to meet the family's needs

Working and Caring for a Child with an ASD

Do you feel you are working full-time at everything? You are. The reality is that no one person can do everything. A single parent has the jobs of parenting, career, and maintaining a home. How can anyone do all of these things and still find time to sleep? The answer is simple: They can't, and you can't either.

Attempting to do everything alone is setting yourself up for failure. You may need to ask friends and family for help.

HAVING AN ORGANIZED SYSTEM

Make your life easier by setting up a realistic schedule. Plan times for baths, medications, stories, and all of the daily and weekly activities in which you and your child engage. If you have a specific time you do things, you will not feel the stress of trying to remember what needs to be done. It is hard to concentrate on reading your child a story if you are simultaneously trying to remember your other tasks. Putting up a poster board with drawings of the activities that you need to do with the corresponding times will help you stay on schedule and help your child know what to expect.

PRIORITY ONE IS TAKING CARE OF YOURSELF

We have been taught in our culture that taking care of yourself is selfish. This is particularly true for mothers who can feel guilty if they cannot be there every moment for their children. These are very normal feelings. However, if you are overwhelmed and stressed, it will be even harder for you to care for your children and run a household, let alone work. Yes, you are a mother, but you are also a human being whose needs must be met in order for you to function and to get some enjoyment from life. Support from an understanding friend or a counselor can help you identify how you can take care of yourself and also care for your children.

PRIORITY TWO IS YOUR JOB

Your second priority is your job. You have responsibilities to your job, and although it is very hard to combine work with the single parenting of a child with a disability, you can do it. The first thing you will want to do is find the most dependable daycare or after-school care possible. It may be a family member or friend—someone in whom you have the utmost confidence.

Talk to your employer about the fact that you have sole responsibility for your child, and that this could infringe on your work hours. Don't be overly dramatic or appear as though you are seeking sympathy. Be matter-of-fact and businesslike. Emphasize that there will be as little interference with your work as possible.

Employers want people who are willing to work hard and deliver quality work. You may find your company is willing to make allowances for employees who have special needs. Split shifts, working from home, and flexible schedules are some of the options that may be available.

PRIORITY THREE IS YOUR CHILDREN

Meeting the needs of all of your children will take a lot of your time. For your child with autism, you will need to work to integrate speech therapy, sensory strategies, behavior management, and self-care skills into everyday life. You may be using a special diet or doing therapy as well as coordinating with the different professionals your child sees regularly. Beyond the needs of this child, your other children will require your attention, care, and guidance. Using your mindfulness practices to slow yourself down and breathe can help when you begin to feel guilty or overwhelmed. You may consider delegating some responsibilities or chores to older children, or even young ones, who would likely enjoy the responsibility for its own sake if not for some reward (e.g., Friday DVD/streaming movie nights, or a stretch of uninterrupted Mom/Dad time on the weekend).

PRIORITY FOUR IS YOUR HOME

You have to accept that there will be times when the house is messier than you would like. It is so easy to be caught up in the trap that the house reflects how well you are doing as a mom or a dad, and it simply isn't true. Slowing down, taking a deep breath, and stepping back can help you assess what is truly important in the moment so you can refocus and shift your priorities.

Tend to the issues that keep the family safe. A clean bathroom and kitchen are important, but if all the towels aren't folded and you need to fetch one from the laundry basket, it's okay. Organize your schedule so that you aren't overwhelmed with a huge mess at the end of the week. Doing a little each night is much easier than trying to do everything on a Saturday.

Simple timesavers can make your life much easier. There are many resources available, such as magazine articles, books, and websites that have tips on how to save time in the house. Research different ideas and use the ones that work for you. As a start, try the following:

○ Lighten up the kitchen chores. Use paper plates.

○ Make mealtime preparation faster. Buy single-serving, ready-to-serve grocery products for your child unless he or she has dietary restrictions.

○ Have at least two weeks' worth of clean underwear, pants, and pajamas for your child so you aren't having to do laundry late at night.

○ If you have a cat, buy a covered litter box. Children with ASD are often intrigued by the cat box.

○ Invest in a new laundry basket. Find one with three compartments to separate laundry during the week to prevent having to sort it all at laundry time.

○ Give yourself a night off once a week. Visit the local fast-food restaurant. It may have a playground where your child can burn off some extra energy in a safe environment.

One great timesaver is paying your bills online. You can create automatic payments for many of your bills on your credit card and then just pay your credit card bill each month. Many banks also have online services with bill-paying features.

THE PARENT AND CHILD TEAM

Enlist your child's help with household chores as soon as he is old enough. Teach him how to use a feather duster. The job won't be done perfectly, but he will thoroughly enjoy the process and it will save some work. Children love to help empty wastebaskets and children with autism are no exception. Teach your child how to make his bed and pick up his own toys.

Doing these little chores will help keep the house clean and allow you and your child to work on something together. You are also helping your child learn some basic life skills that he will use forever.

Finding Reliable Daycare

For the parent of a child with autism, finding reliable daycare may be a challenge. Sometimes a family member can help. Grandparents, aunts, uncles, cousins, siblings, or extended family members are your best options. Talk to members in your support group for additional suggestions. The Health and Human Services office in your area may also have some ideas for options for daycare and respite care. There are alternatives, but they can be difficult to find. You'll need to be persistent. When you start to feel frustrated, take some deep breaths, and slow yourself down to prevent yourself from getting more worked up. Sometimes taking your focus off your search for an answer will allow an answer to come to you when you least expect it!

Word of mouth continues to be the best recommendation, so don't hesitate to ask people you know and trust. When you do get a referral, visit the daycare center several times, and meet with the person who will be caring for your child. If possible, arrive at the daycare unannounced so you can see how things are run when visitors are not expected. Ask for references and contact them. Never place your child in an environment that makes you feel uncomfortable.

Dating and Future Relationships

Many single parents, particularly single moms, are unsure how to approach dating, or even if they should date at all. They are concerned about how a potential serious relationship would affect their child with autism. They are equally concerned about how another adult, who is not the parent, will feel about a child with autism.

DATING

Dating after you have been divorced or widowed can be difficult even for a person without children; it is a major challenge for the single parent of a child who is on the autism spectrum.

Many single parents justify a life of solitude by saying that it is the right thing to do—that they shouldn't bring a stranger into the family if there's a possibility it won't be permanent, or that more time away from the child is a bad idea considering how many hours they already spend at work. Others say they cannot handle both an intimate relationship and the needs of the child.

The Possibility of a Stepparent

When a relationship turns serious, marriage may very well become a possibility. For all practical purposes, whether a couple decides to live together or legally marry, the result is the same. A commitment will be made by two adults to bring their lives together, and this will involve any children in the relationship. It will be of special concern to the parent of a child with autism.

A new partner is also likely to have many concerns, especially if he has no experience with special-needs children. He may worry that he will not know what to do or how to handle this child. He may be concerned about whether he can be an adequate parent to a child he is not entirely sure he understands.

When adults commit to a second marriage and there are children involved, it is wise to talk to a counselor. Many times issues lurking in the background can come to the surface in a discussion with an objective third party, and fears can be put to rest. You can get advice and discuss concerns that either of you may have. It is also a good idea to bring the stepparent-to-be to the child's primary care physician to talk about the child's current and future care.

Invite your future spouse to attend support-group meetings with you. Your new partner can ask questions he or she may not feel comfortable asking you.

The biggest mistake people make is to visualize all the potential problems and situations that could ever possibly come up in an entire lifetime, and imagine them occurring all at once. Remember: Breathe deeply and slow yourself down. You can't solve it all in one day. A counselor can be helpful to voice your worries and help you get some much needed perspective and options.

Concerns of Moms

Once you find a potential mate that you want to share your time with, the first thing you will want to do before introducing him or her to your child is to educate your partner about your child, his strengths and challenges, and his needs and unique traits. Offer this to your partner both in a verbal discussion and give written information about autism that can be read and absorbed over time.

It is important to prepare your partner that your child may not respond positively right away, and to encourage your partner to continue to try to have a relationship with him. Once it is time to introduce your mate and child, please allow your partner to interact with your child alone. Do not hover over them, guide your partner, or observe them by staying in the same room. It is important to give your partner time and space to be with your child alone so the relationship can naturally unfold. You can instruct your partner how to interact with your child, but then you'll need to let go of trying to control how they interact.

If your child is nonverbal, instruct your partner to gently approach him, and to get close to your child so your child will know that he wants to interact with him. Have your partner look your child in the eyes. Even if your child does not give eye contact, have your partner look directly at him. Have your partner softly say hello, smile, and then walk away immediately to give your child his own space again.

Remember, children with autism don't like people too close; however, they do need to have people introduced to them by respectfully moving into their space. After your partner has moved away, it is important for your child to observe you and your mate interacting. This will let your child know that this person is important to you as the mom. Then you can go over and interact with the child to make sure any issues of jealousy or worry of rejection can be addressed.

It is very important for your partner to learn to acknowledge your child and let your child know your partner is there, even if your child doesn't respond right away. Give it time; he will when he feels your partner's respect and care. Gradually build your partner into the family's daily life.

It is very likely you are the custodial parent of your child with autism or perhaps you have joint custody with your ex. Regardless, it is the nature of the mom to feel that as far as her children are concerned, "the buck stops here." The responsibility for these children is not something any parent, mom or dad, takes lightly, but to most mothers it is of critical importance.

If you have joint custody, you have the advantage of some breathing space while your child is with his father. This will enable you to have a social life or even develop a new relationship without involving your child.

Concerns of Dads

One advantage men have is that the biological mother of the child with autism usually has custody. A single dad's schedule is typically more within his control than the schedule of a single mom.

Men who are single fathers of children with autism also have some disadvantages. Women might perceive them as "mom-shopping" to care for their children. A woman might also fear the responsibility of caring for someone else's child with special needs, or worry that a man with the emotional and financial responsibilities involved in raising a child with special needs will be unlikely to want to have more children. She will also worry about having to deal with the presence of an ex-wife, a woman she will have to interact with even after the child becomes an adult.

Important Points to Consider

It is important with single parenting to not lose yourself in the process. It requires a bit more effort, more organization, and a lot of love.

O When you are a single parent, your order of priorities are first yourself, then your job, then your children, and last household maintenance.

O An effective organizational system will allow you to take care of your family and reduce your worry that you may be forgetting to do something important.

O If you tend to fret about potential problems, trying applying your mindfulness practice to breathe deeply and slow yourself down. Remember, you can't solve it all in one day. A counselor can also help you explore new perspectives and options.

O Include your child in household chores. This will teach him new skills and hopefully give you some much needed help!

 **CHAPTER 9**

Responding to Your Other Children's Needs

Autism affects everyone in the family. Perhaps no one feels this effect more than the siblings of the child with ASD. Parents of the child on the spectrum are, understandably, often so wrapped up in the issues surrounding autism that they overlook the ways autism is affecting their other children. It isn't bad parenting; it is human nature. Raising children is a balancing act for parents as they try to meet everyone's needs and provide a complete childhood for each of their children.

Older Siblings

When an older child or a teenager has a new sibling, it is always an adjustment. When autism is diagnosed a couple of years later, this adjustment will be even more challenging. It is important to remember that the older sibling will need your attention, too, and not to forget or put the child with autism's needs over his needs.

NEW CONSIDERATIONS

If there are a significant number of years separating the older sibling from the child with autism, the younger child with autism may not have as much impact on the daily life of the older child. This is especially true if the older child is in high school, for example, and nearly ready to move out of the house to live on his own or to go to college. The older child may not be much involved with the daily trials of living with a child with autism.

However, the older sibling may have some concerns that younger children wouldn't think of. The older child likely recognizes fairly quickly that autism is going to be around for the rest of his life, and he may already be concerned about his role in taking care of his sibling in several years. This will impact not only his life but the life of his future spouse and any children they may have as well.

SLIGHTLY OLDER SIBLINGS

When a child who is two to eight years younger than her older sibling is diagnosed with autism or another spectrum disorder, it can affect the older sibling in several different ways. Children have their own personalities and how they react in a given situation will depend on their age and maturity. There is no universal way children handle issues in their lives, although there are some generalizations that can be made. Typical reactions can include the following:

O A sibling acts as another parent.

O A sibling pulls away from the family.

O A sibling attempts to "make up" for autism by being a "model" child.

- A sibling establishes his own identity through flamboyant behavior.

- A sibling struggles with anxiety or depression.

- A sibling feels resentment toward the child with autism.

Although this list is not all inclusive, most siblings of children with ASD will fall into one of these categories. Autism itself often seems like more than any person can handle emotionally, so parents can be truly overwhelmed by the realization that their other children have developed problems because of their sibling. Your mindfulness practice can be helpful so that you can slow yourself down and deal with one issue, one crisis, and one dilemma at a time.

Children accustomed to their sibling with autism not participating in games are thrilled when interaction and participation begins. They also can become jealous because of the attention focused on the child with autism. Don't forget to praise your other children for their skills and achievements.

THE PARENTAL SIBLING

Children who begin to act as another parent have both positive and negative issues to deal with. The positive side is the child's acceptance and involvement in the family. As that child matures into an adult, he will have compassion for people with disabilities. The downside is that the parents might come to heavily rely on such a child, and the child takes on so much responsibility that he becomes overwhelmed.

Parents need to be vigilant when an older child becomes parental. It isn't a behavior to be discouraged, as families should work together and look out for each other. But it is important not to let a child take on so much responsibility that he loses himself in the process. A child who observes his younger sibling about to poke a fork in an electrical outlet and stops him is a good thing. A child who feels responsible for everything the child with autism does may carry a lifelong burden that could take considerable counseling to resolve.

Teaching Mindfulness to Siblings

How you teach your other children mindfulness will be very different from the method you use with your child with autism, as you will help them become aware and calm by using both language to process their emotions and a meditative process.

In order to help them, you will need to feel comfortable with your own mindfulness practice. Remember, your children are much more likely to do what you are doing, rather than simply following what you say. You will want to make sure that you are not poking fun at or making light of your children's feelings, nor are you trying to fix their problems. You are simply offering them new ways to move through negative emotions as an opportunity for connection with themselves and with you.

STEPS TO MINDFULLY CONNECT WITH YOUR NON-AUTISTIC CHILD

○ *Turn off all distractions* so you can truly listen to your child.

○ *Empathize* by offering soothing words and touch.

○ *Help your child label the emotion* he is feeling, e.g., "You sound really angry right now. Is that how you are feeling?"

○ *Offer guidance on how he can regulate his emotions.* "Would it help you calm down right now if we did some deep breathing together?"

○ *Set limits and teach acceptable expression of emotions and problem-solving skills.* "In the future when you are angry with your sister, another option besides hitting is to take three deep breaths and walk away. Sometimes walking away helps everyone calm down quickly."

○ *Teach your child his own mindfulness meditation practice.* You can teach a child of almost any age how to meditate. If you have your own meditation practice, your child has likely noticed. This can be a great starting point for a conversation. When meditating with children, it is necessary to simplify the practice and keep it short. Five minutes might seem like an eternity to a child, so start small. Invite your child to sit still with you for one minute, breathing and listening. Keep it short and positive, even if your child moves around or breaks the silence. After you've finished meditating, encourage your child's innate curiosity. Guide your child to pay attention to his breath, the sensations of his body, and the activity of his mind. What does he notice when he holds still? Be supportive throughout.

Younger Siblings

Younger children who have a slightly older sibling with autism have much the same issues as those with a slightly younger one, though magnified. Because of the nature of ASD, a child with autism demands more time, patience, and tolerance than a child without the disorder. The problem? The child without the disorder can "get lost." It is so easy to postpone the needs of another child because of the heavy demands of a child with ASD.

Negative attention is better than no attention—or so it may seem to a child. It is especially true for the sibling of a child with autism. If your other children begin having behavior problems, use your mindfulness practice to gently review how much individualized time they get from you so that you can begin to discern how you can balance the attention that your children need.

JEALOUSY AND RESENTMENT

Parents will need to be aware of how to avoid jealousy and resentment from their other children. The teenage years are challenging enough, so it is important for you to watch for signs in your children indicating whether jealousy and resentment are becoming an issue. A child may:

O Request that Mom and Dad attend school functions alone

O Feel concern or embarrassment about having his friends visit for sleepovers or other activities

O Become more in need of physical contact with one or both parents, wanting closeness such as cuddling

O Express jealousy overtly, as with the phrase "But she gets to . . ."

O Argue excessively about chores and responsibilities

O Show behavior that indicates an obsession with his health

COMPETITIVENESS

Watch for signs of competitive behavior between your children. A child who goes out of his way to show parents his accomplishments and skills may be feeling that the child with autism is getting a lot of positive feedback for reaching what is perceived to be very small goals. A child without autism may not understand or care that finally speaking one or two words is an enormous victory, and will not understand why such a fuss isn't made over his normal or above-normal accomplishments. It is important to take the time to praise all of your children for each milestone they accomplish.

Other behaviors will surface that are unique to each child, and the parents are the best gauges of those actions. Using the core practice of slowing down, taking deep breaths, and tuning into your emotions and bodily sensations before you react can guide a parent into a proper course of action. Contrary to what children think, moms and dads usually love their children equally, and it is the job of the parents to display that through their behavior. Use your mindfulness practice to slow down so you can accurately check yourself to be sure you are conveying balanced messages to each member of your family.

Growing Up Too Fast

If there is a child with autism in the family and another baby comes along ten years later, there are some unique issues to be faced by the family. This age gap frequently occurs when parents have put off having a second child because of the pressures associated with raising a child with autism.

When a sibling is much younger than the child with autism, the younger child will never know of any adjustment that had to be made in the family. This is simply life, the way it has always been, and the way it will always be.

Safety is an issue for parents with a newborn. If a child with autism is not totally self-involved, she may be very interested in the new baby. Her curiosity and lack of impulse control could inadvertently cause harm. Parents should take extra safety measures to avoid accidents.

It is very easy to unintentionally cause a child to "grow up" too quickly. Even though they are only several years apart, the younger child starts watching out for the older because it is the natural thing to do. This burden of responsibility is too much for a child to bear, and may be sowing the seeds of resentment that will bloom fully later in life.

Most children realize as they approach their young adult years that the sibling with autism will forever be a part of their life. Realization strikes that caring for this sibling may someday be their responsibility. When your child begins to discuss this topic with you, it would be helpful to use mindfulness principles to help him through this potentially difficult conversation.

When a child is much younger than his sibling with autism, it is less likely that the disability will interfere in the activities of childhood. The family will have adjusted and found their own routine that the younger child will fit into. Having respite care for your child with autism will allow you to have time alone with your younger child.

The Isolated Sibling

Some children will fail to form an attachment to their sibling with autism and may attempt to put as much distance between themselves and their sibling and family as possible. Often the cause is quite simple: These children are tired of living with autism.

It is important that a child who withdraws from the family because of autism be allowed to flourish on his own. These children may be susceptible to depression, and if so a therapist might be needed to address the issues of this child. It is very important that the parents spend time just with that child to enjoy activities and projects that are unrelated to autism. Parents also need to be clear, verbally and through their actions, that they do not feel the sibling is responsible for his sister. The less the child with autism impacts his sibling, the better the chances for both children to evolve a healthy relationship over time.

Support groups for parents of children with autism can provide information on locating a support group for siblings. Check with your local chapter of the Autism Society or other organizations that have support groups. You want your child to feel supported and know that he is not alone.

The Social Impact of Having an ASD Sibling

Children who have a sibling with ASD usually have mixed feelings about their brother or sister. Having a sibling with autism can affect their social life. Like any brother and sister combination, it can be a rocky road laced with arguments and love. The sibling may claim his sister as his worst enemy or best friend, depending on the day.

PEERS

Some of the biggest problems siblings of ASD children face are issues within their own peer group. Your child, having the experience of a sibling with a disability, has a different outlook on the world from that of many children. It is not unusual for children, particularly in the middle and elementary school years, to hear other children tease or outright ridicule their sibling with autism. Parents should address this immediately, as the problem will only escalate and eventually alienate a child from his own peer group.

If a child is being singled out because of his sibling, it is important for the parents to contact the school. In this case, it isn't enough to tell your child to ignore the teasing, for two reasons; your child will generally defend his sibling with autism and be on the defensive whenever interacting with his peer group. Do not hesitate to schedule a conference with counselors, teachers, or other school staff to address and put an end to the problem.

FAMILY EVENTS

You don't always have to keep your children apart. Your children may find that if they include their friends in family activities, their friends will be more accepting of their sibling with special needs than expected. In one instance, a child who has a brother with autism wanted him to attend a concert with her but she was worried about what would happen. Her solution was to have her father sit with her brother next to the exit in case they needed to make a hasty exit.

Don't hesitate to ask your child what he might suggest as ways to solve situations that could arise during social occasions. The goal is to make the other sibling feel comfortable without leaving out the child with autism. Sometimes it is not appropriate to bring a child with autism to certain events and other situations, and then there will be times when your child will be able to calmly participate and enjoy the event.

There is a 3 to 9 percent chance that in a family having one child with autism, a second child will also have autism. In some families, one or two cousins, aunts, and/or uncles may also have ASD.

Considering Future Children

It is difficult, if not impossible, to advise a couple on whether or not they should consider having more children if they already have a child on the autism spectrum. So many factors are involved and it is a very personal decision. It is not a decision a couple can rush into or let others make for them.

GENETICS OR UNKNOWN

If the ASD your child has is a proven genetic disorder, such as Rett Syndrome or Fragile X Syndrome, you may want to consider genetic testing to determine the risk factors for a future pregnancy. If one child has been born with a genetic disorder, the odds are high that another will be as well. In this case, a genetic counselor and perhaps family counseling can help you reach a difficult decision.

MENTAL, EMOTIONAL, AND FINANCIAL IMPACTS

A couple should consider not only the mental and emotional impact of having another child with special needs, but also the financial and long-term issues involved with raising children on the spectrum.

There are government programs to help parents who meet certain guidelines. Supplemental Security Income (SSI) is a program managed by the Social Security Administration. Benefits are paid directly to families to help with the expenses of daily living. Autism is an automatic allowance for benefits if your family meets certain qualifications such as income level and value of assets. Before you apply for SSI, be sure that you have documentation from your pediatrician that thoroughly documents the diagnosis of an autism spectrum disorder.

Regardless of a child's age, the school system should help with early intervention. Even if your child is under school age, contact the school district to find out what programs and resources are available.

It is also important to remember that financial planning must be in place to protect and provide for any children if a parent dies. Life insurance, trust funds, and wills that provide for guardianship of a child are not luxuries. They are necessary and must be kept up-to-date at all times.

IT'S YOUR DECISION

There are many well-meaning people, such as extended family, friends, and in-laws, who often feel it is their place to advise a couple on their family planning. Although it is difficult, you can stress, very kindly, that this is a personal decision and you have handled it. If people persist in advising you against your wishes, be very firm and polite in asserting your right to privacy.

If you are struggling with a decision whether to have more children, you may want to go to counseling to help you sort out your feelings. An impartial third party can be more helpful than those who are close to you, who may mean well but not know the best way to support you.

Important Points to Consider

The siblings of the child with ASD will profoundly feel the impact of having a brother or sister with special needs. Parents of the child on the spectrum are often so wrapped up in the issues surrounding autism that they can overlook the ways autism is affecting their other children.

- O Siblings of a child with autism may have mixed feelings. They may feel protective and at the same time resentful over how much time and energy the parents spend on their sibling.

- O Many siblings grow up too fast when they have a brother or sister with special needs to care for. Be aware of the signs that your other child is struggling.

- O You may want to consider a support group for siblings. Check with your local chapter of the Autism Society or other organizations that have support groups.

- O It is the decision of you and your mate whether or not you would like to have more children when you already have a child on the autism spectrum.

CHAPTER 10

Autism and Your Extended Family

Autism and its related conditions are often misunderstood by the extended family. Some of your relatives may not even have heard of autism, or may have misconceptions about it. Family members will have various responses as they attempt to advise the parents and educate themselves in the process. Understanding common reactions and how to handle them can prevent misunderstandings that are harmful to family relationships from occurring.

Grandparents

Grandparents can be the easiest or the hardest family members to deal with when a child is diagnosed with autism. Most of the time they are a blessing, because of their wisdom and experience and their willingness to assist and provide moral support through the early years of a child's life. Grandparents can be difficult to deal with because they may not understand the child's reactions or the way he communicates, particularly if he is nonverbal. They may be confused by your child's responses because they may be expecting your child to respond the same way that their grandchildren who do not have autism act.

THOSE WHO ARE HELPFUL

Often it is the grandparents that raise the first alert that something is amiss. A grandparent may question whether the child can hear properly. Grandparents generally love and care deeply for their grandchildren, but they are not with the child day in and day out, so they can spot the lack of development more quickly than those who see the child on a daily basis.

Your parents can be your best advocate and stress reducers. Grandma may come through and shine when Mom herself is falling apart over the diagnosis. Grandpa may do what dads do best—try to solve all the problems. If your parents do not live nearby or you just don't relate well to them, perhaps you can receive support from your spouse's parents.

Grandparents may have never heard of autism and may need to be educated about the various problems that come with the condition. You can offer them the FAQ in the appendix of this book, or give them a copy of this book and any other books or articles you have found helpful.

THOSE WHO ARE DIFFICULT

It is extremely hard on families when the grandparents of a child with special needs create difficulties, so if problems exist, it is wise to look for the cause. Generally, one of two issues is at the center.

The most common reason grandparents relate poorly, or not at all, to a grandchild who has special needs is simply that they are baffled. They don't have any idea how they should act, what they should do, whether they should make allowances and, if so, what kind and how much. It can appear as though they are ignoring their grandchild, but the reality is that they are at a loss as to how to handle the situation.

If you have a parent who appears to be ignoring your child because he is unsure of what to do, help him become involved with his grandchild by guiding the way. Model for him how to care for your child and teach him about the communication system. Once he learns how to interact with your child, he will become more confident in that relationship.

Less common, and much more difficult to handle, is the grandparent who chooses not to accept a child with a disability. This is a loss for the child and creates resentment from the child's parents, creating arguments and disharmony within the family. The other children will sense the dissension in the family; they can become tense and insecure. After all, they may wonder, will they be rejected, too, if something happened to make them "less than perfect"?

SOLUTIONS FOR DIFFICULT SITUATIONS

Suggesting the grandparents see a counselor may make things worse. To suggest that your mother or father has a problem may only create anger and bitterness. Most parents who have struggled with this situation have said that only some distance makes things bearable. If putting distance between you and the situation is not possible, limit contact as much as possible. Your other children can still see their grandparents, but explain to the children that the activity or location they are going to visit is not appropriate for your child with autism.

The Unique In-Law Problem

In this case, a problem doesn't exist between the in-laws and the child with autism, but rather between the parents and the in-laws. There are no hard and fast rules on when this problem will occur, but there are some definite trends.

MOM AND HER MOTHER-IN-LAW

When family relationships are strained, the most common problem is between the mother and her husband's mother. Sometimes the relationship with a mother-in-law can be touchy even if there isn't a child with special needs. If the relationship is already strained and a grandchild is diagnosed with autism, a bad situation is exacerbated and the entire family can feel tremendous stress. Mom may find every decision or treatment being questioned by her mother-in-law. Raising a child with autism is challenging enough without having to defend every decision. If you have a problem with your mother-in-law, ask your husband to talk with her, or both of his parents together, to work toward a solution. If he won't, or if it does no good, handle the situation with as much grace as possible and avoid as many interactions as you can. It is not good for you to feel stressed and resentful at every encounter with your mother-in-law. It is also not good for your children; if you are being questioned on decisions and choices you make for your family, it undermines your authority as a parent.

While it is difficult, if either set of parents questions your decisions about your children, you may have to be assertive and not engage in the conversation. When questions are asked, assume they come from a place of concern, but if you feel you are being doubted, stand your ground. Use your mindfulness practice to help you relax before reacting.

DAD AND HIS MOTHER-IN-LAW

The old jokes about in-laws have always centered on a man's mother-in-law, which is usually an unfair commentary on a woman's mother—but when it is a difficult relationship, the jokes ring all too true. This is magnified when a child has a condition and the cause is unknown. Couple that with the lack of any definitive treatment and a tense situation can be the result. The mother may blame autism on genetics, even when no cause has been established—and, of course, it will be the fault of the father of the child because of his bad genes. This is also sometimes used as a justification for saying, "I told you marrying him was a mistake."

When a dad has this problem, his wife needs to talk to her parents. A father of a child with autism has his own issues to deal with as he tries his best to juggle career, kids, and other activities. The last thing he needs to add to his plate is a challenging mother-in-law.

Other Family Members

Mothers-in-law are not the only family members who can make relationships uncomfortable. There are aunts, uncles, cousins, nieces, nephews, and even grandchildren involved in an extended family. And if a family is very large, there will be a great number of people related only by marriage who are involved as well.

THE GOOD

Fortunately, this is the most common situation for parents of children with autism and their extended families. Every family has its trials and tribulations, but when a family can work together for common goals, everyone benefits. If your extended family is supportive and helpful, involve them in activities as much as you can, as it will help your child develop social and interpersonal skills.

THE BAD

Usually when a situation with extended family is not ideal, parents may decide not to participate in family events because they haven't figured out how to manage autism easily or because they feel unwelcome. If you consider your extended family ties to be less than ideal, try to figure out why. Is it possible that no one knows what to say to you or how to act with your child? Education about autism can make the unknown less intimidating. Ignoring the issues won't change them or make them go away, but addressing them directly can improve the situation.

THE UGLY

Situations between family members can become very ugly when people have negative feelings toward one another and feel a need to express those feelings. This is especially true when there may be unresolved personal issues that are not being addressed, so it becomes easier to focus on the child with autism. Sometimes family members can say hurtful or negative things about your parenting style, your choices, or your decisions.

If the relationships in your family are hostile or saturated with bad memories, you may not be able to work through the situation. Your first priority is your own family, and you have to do what is necessary to protect and care for them.

Celebrating Family Holidays

It seems that just about the time you have established a routine that works, a holiday comes along. Coping with holidays can include extensive planning and setting up alternatives in case problems arise, but it is well worth the effort to make these days more fun for your family.

SPRING AND SUMMER HOLIDAYS

There are several holidays during the warmer weather that are usually enjoyed by families. Having a child with autism does not mean that you have to stop enjoying these events. Be aware of and plan for situations that may overstimulate your child so you can prevent problems. For example, Easter can involve egg hunts outdoors with crowds and excessive movement by other children that can feel overwhelming to your child. Mother and Father's Day may involve parties with extended family. Your child may be confused why the family is getting together and celebrating an event where there are no decorations or activities to help him understand the event, such as Halloween or Christmas. Independence Day can be extremely overstimulating as many activities involve large crowds and loud fireworks.

AUTUMN HOLIDAYS

For most children, there is only one holiday in the fall that matters: Halloween. October 31st is a day to dress up and collect candy. Many children with autism do not like Halloween, because of difficulties wearing the costumes and the confusion from all the stimulation and activity.

How does a parent explain to a child who is struggling with communication and conceptual skills not to take candy from a stranger, but then allow the child to march up to a strange doorway and ask for candy? If a child is on a special diet to treat autism, how do you explain to that child that all the other children get candy, but he doesn't? And how do you keep your own little goblin straight in a swarm of ghosts, bogeymen, and skeletons?

Unfortunately, there are no easy answers. Some parents only take their children trick-or-treating in a controlled environment, such as a shopping mall. Others go only to the homes of people they know, and others find it easier to avoid the holiday bustle.

WINTER HOLIDAYS

Although many holidays change our daily routines, there are none quite like those from Thanksgiving to New Year's. The activities that the holidays bring can turn a child's world topsy-turvy. For a child with autism, the change in routine is not only unwanted, it is upsetting and can cause behavioral issues.

Some of the events that arise during the holiday season can be upsetting for the child with autism. Some unusual events include:

O Parents may go to parties, meaning that a babysitter will be needed.

O The other children will want their annual visit to Santa for photographs and wish-list sharing.

O Friends and family may pop in for visits unannounced.

O Carolers, a total mystery to a child with autism, may show up outside your front door.

O The time spent in stores and shopping malls is greatly increased as families buy presents. The crowds, holiday decorations, and mall activity can be very confusing for your child.

- Regularly watched television shows may be pre-empted for Christmas programs.

- School is out of session during winter vacation for up to two weeks.

- There is a sudden influx of gifts, a decorated tree, and holiday baking.

Try to involve your child in ways that he can enjoy—for instance, decorating the tree. It may be the most unusual and perhaps bizarre tree you will ever see, but it is a delightful and memorable way to celebrate.

As the holidays get into full swing, remember that children with autism, depending on their abilities, have their own special talents and abilities that they can contribute, like creating decorations, making holiday cards, hanging decorations and lights on the tree, making centerpieces for the table, etc., and even though their creations may not be traditional in nature, they are things of beauty, things to be treasured, and remembered for a lifetime.

When overstimulation becomes an issue, the best advice a parent can follow is to "go with the flow." Plan ahead—don't visit Santa during the busiest part of the weekend, and perhaps buy most of your gifts online or order from catalogs. Trust yourself and follow your instincts; if your child appears to be overstimulated or agitated, slow things down.

Special Occasions

Even families with non-ASD children can be challenged by the interactions and activities of special social occasions. Some of these events can be especially problematic for a child with autism because of their high levels of stimulation and emotional charge.

If at all possible, continue attending family events. Interacting with the child with autism at these events will help both the immediate family and the farther-flung relatives feel involved and ultimately more comfortable with the situation. Plan ahead and prepare so these events can be positive for everyone involved.

> If a family member has passed away, particularly one who was close to your child, alert your child's teacher and therapists. Your child may exhibit behaviors that will surprise everyone if they are not aware of the situation. Children with autism may not directly express their grief, but it is present.

FUNERALS

A death in the family can present unique concerns. Because concepts are difficult to understand for people with autism, and death is a difficult concept for anyone to understand, your child with autism may be troubled by a funeral. Acting-out behaviors are common in these situations. Funerals are often disturbing even to children who do not have autism, so leaving all the younger ones with a babysitter may be the best idea.

Explaining Conscious Parenting to Extended Family

It may help to explain to your extended family why you have chosen to consciously parent your children. As you know, some family members will understand and others will not. It may be particularly challenging for your parents or grandparents to understand conscious parenting principles, as they are accustomed to the old parenting paradigm. Your parents may be concerned that you are not providing enough structure or firm guidance. You can explain that conscious parenting is not allowing the children a free-for-all, but it is providing firm boundaries along with communication, choices, and opportunities to help them make better decisions. This may not make much sense to them, so use your discernment on when to stop, particularly if you feel like you are having to justify your parenting style. If you start feeling overwhelmed by the discussion, you can breathe deeply, slow yourself down, and choose to respectfully end or redirect the discussion.

Important Points to Consider

Extended family can be a wonderful support or cause of great frustration when raising your child with autism. When you understand potential common reactions from family members, you can determine how to best handle these reactions and how to effectively communicate to prevent further misunderstanding.

○ You may need your mindfulness practice of breathing and slowing down when dealing with your family. Knowing how to step back before reacting can be very helpful.

○ Be aware of the risk of overstimulation during the holiday season. If the noise and bustle get to be too much, have a plan in place so you can calmly and easily leave a situation before a meltdown occurs.

○ There may be some family events that are more low-key that your child with autism will enjoy, while other events that have a high emotional charge may be more difficult to handle.

○ Your family may be concerned that you are choosing to consciously parent, simply because they do not understand what it involves. Explain to them that it is not allowing the children a free-for-all, but it is providing firm boundaries along with communication, choices, and opportunities to help them thrive.

**CHAPTER 11**

Dealing with Society

Parents of a child with autism are very familiar with their child's behavior. Society, however, is still not accustomed to these unusual reactions. Though the number of diagnosed autism cases has increased, many people have not had direct interactions with people with autism. The majority of the children do not look as if they have special needs, so when they begin to exhibit bizarre or out-of-control behaviors, it can create a great deal of discomfort for some people.

Shopping

As mentioned earlier, one of the biggest challenges a family faces with a child with autism is the sometimes-dreaded shopping trip. The weekly grocery shopping is necessary, but a trip to the mall is often considered more trouble than it is worth.

THE GROCERY STORE

It is always an adventure to go grocery shopping with children, and this is especially true with a child with special needs. Kids with autism know what they like. And what they like, they want. And when they want it, they want it now!

You might think that the easiest way to avoid the grocery store trauma is to avoid taking your child at all. How much easier is it for you to have your spouse watch her or to hire a babysitter? But there is a practical side to taking your child grocery shopping, even though it is harder for you. Shopping is a basic skill that needs to be learned, and it often takes years for a child with autism to learn how to shop and to master this necessary skill for adult independence.

If a child with autism wants something in a grocery store, she will simply put it in the shopping cart. She may not even know what it is, but the colors or shapes attract her. Watch while your groceries are being checked out so that you don't accidentally buy unwanted merchandise!

Involving your child in shopping is one way to prevent battles over what goes into the grocery cart. For example, if you are going to buy a dozen apples, have your child select them and put them into a bag. As she is choosing the apples, guide her and show her that one has a bruise and isn't what you want, so she can learn. As she fills the cart, keep an eye on items such as bread that might get squashed, and help her arrange the cart.

She may not seem to be taking it all in, but she is, and she will learn each time she visits the store with you.

A useful trick a parent can adopt to keep a shopping trip under control is to bring small, inexpensive toys for the child to play with. Handheld puzzles, travel toys, and action figures are great choices. If the child is small enough to be in the cart, she can hold and play with these toys. If she is pushing the cart, the toys can be attached to the handle. Giving her something to feel will help her know where to keep her hands and focus.

THE DISCOUNT SHOPPING STORE

Shopping in the huge one-stop discount store is a particular challenge. While everything you could want is under one roof, it takes little time for a child to realize that the store contains many things *she* wants. These yearnings coupled with the huge amount of sensory information surrounding shoppers in these stores can be a recipe for meltdowns and frazzled parents.

The lights are fluorescent, and it is common for children with autism to see the blinking and flashing that most people cannot perceive. There are also many bright and colorful items within the store that will rush into your child's visual processing center all at once. Noise from the intercom systems, other children, and crowd chatter may be painful for your child's ears.

THE SHOPPING MALL

Shopping malls are a mixture of good news and bad news. The good news is that there is enough to keep a child entertained, and the bad news is that, like other kinds of shopping, your child is likely to be overstimulated. Some children enjoy listening to music in headsets to help reduce the effects of stimuli in shopping malls. Other children benefit from wearing noise-canceling headphones to reduce the amount of sound they pick up in large, noisy areas.

If your child has a service dog, that dog is legally entitled to go anywhere. If you are denied access, speak with a manager. Be certain that the dog is trained well; he helps your child and you have become an ambassador for the benefits of a service animal.

School Functions

There are two types of school functions parents may have to deal with when they have a child on the autism spectrum: those that involve the child and those that involve the child's siblings. Each offers opportunities for positive reinforcement as well as the potential for some difficulties.

IN THE SPOTLIGHT

If your child is in special education, she may not be involved in many school functions such as concerts and plays. But if your child is in inclusive education, meaning that she has classes with the rest of her classmates along with some special education classes for specific needs, there will be more occasions for after-school functions. Many children with autism have an aptitude for music and do well in a school band. If your child participates in band and is able to function as part of the greater whole, it will be tremendously rewarding for her, as well as for you. The steps of progress may be slower for the child with autism, but the joy felt as progress is made is a feeling like no other!

IN THE AUDIENCE

Much more commonly, your child will attend her siblings' school functions with you. Concerts, plays, band recitals, and athletic events are only some of the functions you will probably attend over the years. Sometimes your child with autism will enjoy them, and it will be a pleasurable experience for everyone.

Following much of the previous advice will be helpful for school functions. There is a lot of noise and activity when school-age children get together. There is also a great potential for sensory overload. Centering your child's mind on her music or wearing sound-canceling headsets (as described previously) can be helpful. Having paper to draw or color on will provide a better experience for everyone involved. If the activity is something that your child enjoys, you will find her watching with great interest, and so much the better. This may become an interest for her to pursue as well.

Consider bringing a sitter to school functions to be in charge of handling any situations that arise with your child, or to act if your child needs to be quickly removed from the audience. This will allow you to continue watching your other children's performances.

If an event does not turn out to be a total success, don't throw in the towel. Try again another time, being sure to sit near the exit ready to make a quick dash if the experience is less than interesting for your child.

Restaurants

Eating out in restaurants can be a challenge for the parents of a child with autism. That doesn't mean you should never do it. You can still eat out at restaurants and enjoy yourself and your child with autism. You will most likely have to make a few modifications to your plans, and be prepared for anything like needing to eat quickly, sitting in the quietest part of the restaurant away from the crowds and excessive movement, and having your child sitting with her back against the wall so she will feel safe.

It would be wise to choose a child-friendly restaurant and to go early, and not on a Saturday night. This way there will be minimal noise and faster service. Talking about where you are going or showing your child pictures of a family eating in a restaurant could be helpful. Bring along a favorite toy and a book.

GO OUT FOR DINNER!

Keep in mind some basic strategies for dining out. Don't let any fear of your child's potential meltdown keep you from the things and places you enjoy. You can increase everyone's enjoyment of the experience if you:

○ Choose a booth whenever possible, and have your child take an inside seat to prevent her from bolting.

○ Bring toys or games that she enjoys to keep her occupied before the meal comes or when she is finished.

○ Order what your child loves and what you know she will eat to prevent tantrums.

○ To prevent spillage, request that no extra glasses of water be brought to the table.

○ Have plenty of napkins available in case something is spilled.

○ Remove salt, pepper, and all other condiments from your child's reach.

○ If your child is exceptionally hungry, request a side dish of food to be served immediately to raise her blood sugar or give her a snack before you leave for the restaurant.

○ Don't let dessert items be brought to the table until everyone, including your child, has finished the main meal.

○ Don't worry about food spilled on your child's clothes; in the scheme of things, it is minuscule.

Vacations

Most families take a vacation once every year or two. Many parents of children with autism think that autism precludes them from traveling, but this isn't true. Vacations may pose challenges, but you can plan for and figure out how to prevent or solve problems. When planning your vacation, always remember that your goal is to protect your child, not become so panicked that no one can enjoy the vacation.

There are two things to remember as you plan your vacation. First, you want to maintain the routine of your child as much as possible. Second, maintaining the routine is probably going to be difficult. That may sound like a contradiction, but it is important for parents to remember that they should plan for the best, but be prepared to handle anything unusual that arises.

THE IMPORTANCE OF ROUTINE

People with autism thrive on, and depend on, their routine. Schedules are seldom deviated from, the order in which things are done is consistent, and the way the day unfolds is predictable. While some children adapt well to a disruption in their routine, other children will not adapt at all, and behavioral problems can be the result.

Keep as much of that routine the same as you can. Getting up and having breakfast at normal times will start the day off on a better foot when the family is away. If your child is used to watching television in the morning, and you are in a motel or hotel with a TV, turn it on and find her favorite programs. If you are camping, find an activity that will distract her from dwelling on her routine. Some families always go to the same child-friendly vacation spot, so their child with autism will be comfortable in the surroundings and look forward to the trip.

AIRPLANE TRAVEL

A trip by airplane may not be the best choice for a child who is prone to temper tantrums or meltdowns. However, if it is a necessity, some suggestions can help you keep things calm and positive.

First, check with the airlines to see if you can be permitted to board ahead of the other passengers. Having a picture schedule laying out the sequence of events or reading a book about an airplane trip may help your child, since she can visualize the airport and airplane.

Favorite small toys, a favorite pillow or blanket, snacks, and a small DVD player with some cartoons or a movie could save the day!

How can I keep some semblance of a normal routine on vacation? One way to do this is to provide favorite meals. Eating is a big sensory experience and meals are pivotal parts of the day. If your child is used to having a grilled cheese sandwich or hamburger and fries at lunch, don't offer fish and chips instead.

Another wise idea would be to check with your child's pediatrician or child neurologist to see if some sedation should be prescribed in case your child needs help with calming down during the flight. There is no concern for flying in particular for autism; however, your child may feel overwhelmed with the changes to her routine and all of the sensory stimuli. Be sure that it is a medication you have tried before the trip in case she reacts adversely.

USING A VACATION AS SENSORY THERAPY

Although a vacation is a time to "get away from it all," your child will still have autism. Incorporating different activities can provide sensory therapy for your child that she might not have otherwise experienced. Don't burden yourself with the idea of therapy; consider it as having fun with your child.

Textures, sounds, sights, colors, and music are just some of the examples. Going to the beach and playing with sand is sensory therapy, and so is walking through a forest and feeling the different varieties of leaves. Museums provide opportunities to identify colors and shapes. Your entire vacation is one big sensory supply package that can be used to provide therapeutic experiences and a lot of fun.

Try to keep your child's sleep schedule and the pace of her day the same as they are at home. Most people tend to burn the candle at both ends on vacation, packing as much fun and activity as possible into their time. If your child is exhausted, difficult behaviors will escalate, and the entire family will feel stressed.

A SPECIAL MEMORY SCRAPBOOK

A project that will keep a child occupied and busy, as well as create a special memory, is a vacation scrapbook. Purchase nontoxic glue and a scrapbook with heavy pages. It is also helpful to have clear double-sided tape, glitter, stickers, and colorful markers. On the cover put your child's name and a photograph of the vacation spot you are going to visit.

During your vacation, help your child collect leaves, flowers, brochures, wrappers, photos, and other items of interest. Pasting or taping them into the scrapbook is a tactile experience and will journal the vacation. If your child is nonverbal, she can point to the mementos to let you know what she is thinking about.

A good idea is to take photographs of the family during the vacation and then put them into the book with everyone's names written next to the pictures.

BRINGING THE VACATION HOME

It is also fun on an outdoor vacation to bring along an empty coffee can to collect pebbles and rocks. Rocks have different colors and textures; collecting them can provide a sensory exercise. It is also fun. At the ocean, your child can gather a variety of shells. No matter where you go, it is likely that something can be collected and used for a sensory exercise that also brings your child a lot of pleasure.

Collecting postcards can help her remember the places the family visited on vacation. Punching a hole in the upper corner of each card and attaching them together with a ring or key chain makes these cards easy to view and talk about. This will allow you and your child to look at the cards and remember your vacation together.

Important Points to Consider

Many people have not had direct interactions with children with autism and can be critical of your parenting style. Using mindfulness principles may help you when you feel judged by others when you are out in public. It can be difficult to take your child in public when you are concerned about strangers' reactions, but it is very important that you and your child do not isolate and do participate in daily activities, for the sake of your child and your entire family.

- O Involving your child in shopping is one way to prevent battles over what goes into the grocery cart.

- O Attach toys to the cart or provide your child with handheld puzzles, travel toys, and action figures during shopping. Giving her an object to hold will help her know where to keep her hands and focus.

- O Maintain as much of your home routine as you can during a vacation. Doing so will help your child feel calm.

- O During your vacation, help your child collect items of interest and organize them in a scrapbook as a record of the trip. If your child is nonverbal, she can point to the mementos to let you know what she is thinking about.

 **CHAPTER 12**

Starting School

The first day of school is always exciting for both parents and children. For the parent of a child with autism, daily trips to school have probably been occurring before kindergarten. In the United States, all fifty states are mandated to have early intervention programs and special education available to children. For children with autism, early intervention will most likely begin when reasons for concern are detected, which will lead to special education at the age of three.

What You Need to Know about the Law

The special education maze is complicated, and you may sometimes feel as if you are in an adversarial relationship with the school system. You'll want to use your mindfulness centering practice frequently as you learn how to calmly be your child's most effective advocate. Staying informed about political and legal issues that affect children with autism is critical. If you find it hard to speak up when you meet with school personnel, it is wise to take an advocate with you to the meetings, such as a special education attorney or a more experienced parent of a child with autism who may be willing to help.

IDEA

In the mid-1970s, a new law was enacted called the Education for All Handicapped Children Act of 1975. The federal government had finally recognized that inadequate education for children with disabilities was very costly for American society. In 1990, the law was renamed the Individuals with Disabilities Education Act (IDEA), and in 1997, IDEA was given a major facelift and updated again in 2004. Title I is a federal funding program for public schools above a specific student population count. IDEA requires public schools receiving Title I funding to follow two standards: All students must have available to them a free appropriate public education (FAPE), and that education must be within the least restrictive environment (LRE). This education is to be provided from ages three to twenty-two, but may have variances based on individual state laws.

THE LEGALESE OF SPECIAL EDUCATION

Although it may feel as though you need to be an attorney to understand the technicalities of the government's involvement with special education, it isn't all that difficult. Laws will come and go, change and modify, and evolve to better (it's hoped) serve our children. What is important is that you understand the basic principles of special education laws so that when changes do occur, as a parent you can interpret the effect they may have on your child.

Many newsletters and websites exist that provide current and up-to-date information on government issues pending in federal, state, and local legislatures. You don't need to understand or be aware of every little detail, but you do want to know what the law is, or where to find it, should you have problems with your child's education. Avail yourself of all the experts to stay current on congressional activities that affect the rights of students with disabilities.

Integration and Special Education

For children with special needs, education includes much more than the three Rs. Beyond academic learning, students in special education programs also learn about managing the needs of their daily lives. Activities of daily living (ADL) such as self-feeding, dressing, going to the bathroom, and other hygiene needs are also taught. Thus, a multifaceted program, coordinated by teachers, administrators, therapists, and parents, is planned annually. This plan is known as the Individualized Education Program (IEP), which is discussed in more detail in the next section.

LEAST RESTRICTIVE ENVIRONMENTS, MAINSTREAMING, AND INCLUSION

IDEA establishes that students must have access to an education in the least restrictive environment (LRE). In practice, this means that a student must be placed in the same classroom he would attend if he did not have special needs. Supplementary services, such as aides, support systems, and communication equipment, should be used to achieve this goal. If a student's IEP clearly shows that the regular classroom is not suitable, after thoroughly researching the use of various supports, aides, and paraprofessionals, other arrangements can be made. Inclusion, mainstreaming, and LRE all refer to the same thing.

IDEA has recognized that the regular classroom is not suitable for all students. It calls for a "continuum of alternative placement options" to answer the needs of each child. This includes special education classrooms, special schools, or instruction in the home environment. In some instances a personal aide may also be necessary and would be required by law.

ACHIEVING FREE APPROPRIATE PUBLIC EDUCATION (FAPE)

FAPE is something to which every child in the United States is entitled, even if it is a phrase very few parents know. Every child is entitled to have the best education possible; it must be easily accessible, and can have no attached fees. This includes services such as special education and "related services" necessary to fulfill the IEP goals. This mandate applies to all Title I schools and encompasses academics, physical education, speech therapy when needed, and occupational and physical therapy if these have educational benefits.

IDEA says that no child shall be denied needed services because of lack of personnel. If a school does not have the necessary professionals, it is required by law to pay for outside services. You may need to be assertive and have an advocate help you to get the school district to pay for outside services.

These services are always provided and paid for by the state where the child resides. They are mandated by the federal government. Related services relevant to FAPE include hearing evaluations, speech therapy, psychological counseling, physical and occupational therapy, recreational therapy, and vocational counseling. This is not an all-inclusive list, as any service necessary for a child's success is included in this category. These are not luxuries; they are essential to acquiring the free and appropriate public education that every child is entitled to, by law, in the United States. However, when there are state and local budget problems, you may find that you will have to push hard to get needed services and then will have to constantly check to be sure your child is receiving them. "The squeaky wheel does get the grease."

A free and appropriate public education means that every child with a disability should be in essentially the same environment that he would be in if he did not have special needs. Least restrictive environments are part of this education, and related services are as well. FAPE and LRE (or inclusion, as it is commonly known), are the tangible manifestations of IDEA.

Individualized Education Program

The Individualized Education Program (IEP) is the road map that will take your child from early intervention through graduation. This plan describes in detail all special education services that will be called upon to meet the needs of your child with autism. Each IEP is different, because each student is different. It outlines goals and expectations for your child and gives you an idea of what to expect for the school year.

Can a parent ask for a new IEP at any time? Yes. A parent has the right to call for an IEP meeting any time she feels there are needs to be addressed or revisions that should be made. Children change over a twelve-month period and the IEP may need to change as well.

The IEP is a fluid plan, meaning that it changes from year to year and sometimes even within the same year as different milestones are reached or as problems occur. It can also be thought of as a contract, as it commits the school to using resources to achieve the goals the team sets. A well-written IEP eliminates misunderstandings by any of the members of the educational team. Without an IEP, your child does not qualify for special education, so consider this document as a very important part of your child's education.

Traditionally, short-term goals are part of every IEP. Long-term or annual goals in the IEP—the heart of the document—will be the baseline on which a child's education is planned. The goals that are to unfold over a twelve-month period must be reasonable, practical, and designed to strengthen a weak area that is of educational concern. It is important that these goals match the student's current level of performance; they should not reach too high or too low. Parents and teachers need to consider a child's abilities and how they can best enhance those for progress and maturity.

THE IEP TEAM

The IEP team is made up of a group of people who work with you and your child to create the best education plan possible. Certain people are required to be involved. Other experts may be involved as well. The team includes:

O **The student**—Depending on your child's level of functioning, he may be included in an IEP meeting. The team may ask your child some questions, and if your child has difficulties answering these questions, you may help explain his desires and concerns.

O **The special education teacher**—This individual will be the one to oversee the plan that is established in the meeting.

O **A school administrator**—This will be either a principal or a special education director.

O **An adult-service-agency representative**—This is only required if transition services are being planned that would involve an outside agency. If it is physically impossible for someone to attend, a phone conference will suffice. Transition services prepare a special needs child for life after school. This may include preparing the child to live on his own, adaptive skills, exposing the student to a variety of job-related experiences, taking into account the student's interests and/or higher education. These services are generally provided up to the age of twenty-one years (unless your state provides for a longer period of time), and focus on helping the student to be able to meet his goals and objectives upon graduation from high school.

O **An interpreter**—An interpreter is required if the parents are deaf or do not speak English.

Other teachers and therapists may be asked to join the meeting if appropriate. Parents may also request an advocate of their choosing if they wish. An advocate is selected, hired, and paid for by the parent. The school system does not provide an advocate for the parents, as they are not part of the IEP team. It is very helpful to have an advocate, particularly if you are new to the IEP process. Parents must be notified of an IEP meeting reasonably ahead of time, and if the date cannot be arranged with their schedules, the IEP must be rescheduled. If a parent is unable to attend—for instance, because she is serving in the military—the school is to make alternative arrangements through a phone conference or another satisfactory method that will include the parent. An IEP meeting can also be taped if you give the school personnel adequate (at least twenty-four hours) notice that you intend to do this.

The IEP meeting cannot take place without the legal guardian. Parents cannot appoint someone to go in their place, but can have a family member, friend, advocate, or a private professional working with the child accompany them to the IEP meeting. Parents need to be involved and the school district must go out of its way to include them. It is now possible to have an IEP using video conferencing, but it much more effective to have a meeting where all the involved professionals can be present.

THE IEP PROCESS

Your first IEP meeting may be intimidating. You will want to prepare yourself as much as possible and your mindfulness practice can help you manage your anxiety. You can also do this technique during the meeting, taking three breaths so you can slow down and stay as calm as possible. A conference is usually called by the school, but can be called by anyone who feels a meeting is necessary. If a parent requests the IEP, IDEA states that it must be conducted within thirty days from the date the request was filed with the special education department.

IEP meetings take place at the school or a school district office and will include the entire IEP team. This includes parents, teachers, administrators, and anyone involved (even a member of the lunchroom staff isn't out of the question if a child has dietary issues). The entire process can be unsettling to parents, as this large and structured meeting can emphasize the severity of their child's disorder. Again, your mindfulness practices will be really important to help you get through this meeting and also to keep your eye on your child's positive attributes, which may be overlooked while the focus is on solving problems. This team has been created to help your child acquire the best education possible, and you are a team member—with equal ranking and qualification.

As a permanent record, all parties will sign paperwork acknowledging the meeting date and time and you will sign a form acknowledging that you have a copy of the special education laws and that you know your rights and the rights of your child.

The meeting itself will cover all of the team's goals and expectations for your child. You and the team will go through various categories of his education, such as communication skills, and rate his current levels of performance. Goals will then be established to work on for the next twelve months. This process will continue for each service your child needs.

Schools may have their school psychologist do any necessary testing. However, school psychologists may have time and experience limitations. It could be important to have an outside child psychologist do testing to decide which services your child needs and the best way he can learn. If you do not have an official diagnosis and intervention at school is being delayed, consult with a child psychologist, a pediatrician with a special interest in autism, or a developmental pediatrician.

It is helpful for parents to bring a list of questions and goals to the IEP meeting. If you feel the school should provide particular services, this is the place to discuss it. Even if the school personnel do not agree with your requests, they must address them. For example, a school that will not provide sign language instruction at the parent's request needs to have a very good reason for denying it. A speech therapist should be present to talk about the reasons for and against it. Lack of personnel or schedule concerns do not justify not providing services. If you do not agree with the findings decided on at the IEP meeting, it is not necessary for you to sign the IEP plan; or you can sign it but write your objections next to the items with which you disagree.

The IEP meeting should be held every twelve months. As it comes time to plan the next year's IEP, parents should think about the progress their child has made over the past twelve months. Step back and observe your child's behavior, speech, and social skills. Be as objective as possible. If you feel he is progressing at the rate expected, you know the IEP is working. If he isn't progressing, the IEP needs to be revisited with changes made to help your child. If parents move to another school district, the previous IEP should stay in place until a new IEP or testing has taken place. A change of school district requires a new IEP meeting so the parents or guardians and staff are introduced to each other and goals are set. A move does not require new testing.

Reports from professionals in private practice who have examined your child can be read and discussed at the IEP meeting. You may have to be quite assertive to make this happen, as school authorities may be uncomfortable including the report of a private child psychologist who has tested your child. If you feel this information will positively contribute to the care and education of your child, it is your right to include it in the IEP.

Further Education

When your child reaches the age of fourteen, under the IDEA law a school must begin to make a transition plan for your child. This is called an Individual Transition Plan (ITP). The first half of a transition plan is to determine your teen's goals. If your child is able to communicate his hopes for his future, these should be part of the transition plan. The second half addresses how the school will provide an education that will assist your child in meeting those goals. Any needed transition services must be written into the IEP, including a plan for how the goals will be met. You can invite individuals from outside agencies or community organizations to the meeting. In your teen's senior year, a counselor from your state's vocational rehabilitation agency can be invited to assist in planning for job training or any special college programs. Transportation needs should also be addressed.

IDENTIFYING YOUR CHILD'S INTERESTS

As children reach their teenage years, most start expanding their horizons to include special interests. This can also be true for teens with autism, if they have direction and supervision to help them explore the possibilities. It's important that parents help develop interests and talents in their teen so that he has a future with positive opportunities for fulfillment.

How do you determine the interests and talents that may be hidden in your child? You may discover that he has a talent in graphic arts, or that math is second nature to him. Many people with high-functioning autism can successfully find their way into technology fields.

Including your child in activities you are involved in will introduce him to a range of possible interests for himself. He can garden with you, file movies and books, help you paint a wall, or wash the car. Anything you do is something your child might be interested in, and it will give him a bigger window to see what is possible for him to do in the world.

THE TRADITIONAL EDUCATIONAL PATH

Some children with autism continue with traditional education throughout their school career. They may go on to college and become very successful in a chosen field. Having autism does not preclude a college education and a career. Some people with autism have earned their doctorate degrees and become leaders in their field.

Two methods used to instruct children with autism are Treatment and Education of Autistic and Related Communication-Handicapped Children (TEACCH) and applied behavior analysis (ABA). There are supporters and detractors of each method; neither method is right or wrong, as what works for one child may not be suitable for another child. Parents need to understand both methods and decide which is best for their child.

THE TEACCH METHOD

TEACCH is the most commonly used method for the instruction of students with autism. Your school system may not use the term TEACCH for the structure they have in the classroom, but it is easily identified. It teaches according to how the autistic mind works so it is less stressful.

The basis of TEACCH is visual learning and structure. Visualization is a powerful tool for people with autism and can be used in a child's learning. TEACCH uses schedules that are posted in various locations to help a child associate a picture with an activity; this helps with learning the usefulness of words as well as in creating a reliable routine. You can learn more about the TEACCH program on their official website: *www.teacch.com*.

THE ABA METHOD

ABA was developed using the principle of positive reinforcement. Skills are taught to a child and when the skill is performed correctly, the child is rewarded, reinforcing the desired behavior, skill, or activity. Chapter 6 covers ABA therapy in more detail.

Bullying

When a child seems different or is not able to defend himself, he may be a target for bullying. If your child comes home with bruises or seems unusually upset, bullying could be the problem. The first step would be to talk to your child's siblings and any of your child's friends. If you cannot get answers, talk with the teacher or classroom aide. If that is not satisfactory, you might volunteer for a few lunchtime shifts on the playground so that you can observe firsthand what might be going on. If you still don't have definite proof of bullying, speak with the school principal. If the bullying continues, you may need to request an IEP with an advocate or even a special education attorney present.

Bullying can be very damaging and can occur both in and out of school. Your instincts as a parent should let you know that bullying might be occurring, so don't be afraid to be aggressive in finding out what is going on. Sometimes, too, a teacher or an aide can bully a child. This can be a delicate situation. If you hear reports that a staff member is treating your child unfairly, contact or meet with the school administration first so they are aware of your concerns. Document your conversations, in case administration does not adequately deal with the situation. Then you will have a paper trail to substantiate your conversations in case it becomes necessary to have a classroom or even school change.

Knowing your child is being bullied can be very upsetting to a parent, as you watch the impact on your child. You may see your child sad, angry, frustrated, or have an increase in their aggression if they are being bullied. Applying your mindfulness technique can help you stay calm when you become concerned or before you react.

Parents' Expectations

If you can get through your child's time at school without at least one major battle with the school administration and staff each year, you will have the respect and envy of every parent of a child with autism. Keeping your goals and expectations positive and realistic can minimize the battles.

There is a new PTA for you to join. Not the one at your child's school but the one that stands for: *Parent Teacher Advocate.*

You have by now earned the right to use all three titles. You know you are a parent, and you may have figured out that you are your child's first and best teacher. You are also your child's best, and sometimes only, advocate. Running interference is just part of being a parent, though it may be the first line appearing in the job description of a parent of a child with autism.

Important Points to Consider

You will be your child's *Parent Teacher Advocate.* You know your child best and may have to spend time running interference with the school system to make sure your child gets his needs met.

○ In the United States, states are mandated to have early intervention programs and special education available to children. For children with autism, early intervention will most likely begin when reasons for concern are detected, leading to special education starting at the age of three.

○ The IEP (Individualized Education Program) will be the foundation for special education services for your child.

○ Two methods used to instruct children with autism are Treatment and Education of Autistic and Related Communication-Handicapped Children (TEACCH) and applied behavior analysis (ABA).

○ Including your child in activities you are involved in can give both you and your child ideas of his interests and will give you opportunities to see what is possible for him to do in the world.

CHAPTER 13

The Transition from Child to Teenager

Puberty, teenagers, adolescence. These are words many parents dread, and it is no different for the parent of a child with autism. Many of the issues that arise during the teen years bring up questions and concerns that may be difficult to solve. However, because so much has been learned about autism in recent years, more information is available to make this time in a family's life easier. Teenage years can be fun for teens with autism as well.

Physical Changes of Puberty

Puberty! That word can send chills up and down the backs of even experienced parents! It is a time of changes, of testing the boundaries; a time of becoming mature, but acting immature; and a time of experiencing the world. For a teen with autism it is all those things and more. Many changes happen to a teen with autism when puberty arrives. Some are physical and others are emotional and mental.

AUTISM-RELATED CHANGES

If a teen is prone to seizures, this time in her life will likely indicate the role seizures will play in her future. If she has not had seizures previously, she may begin to have them at puberty. If she already has them, they may increase—or could cease. If the frequency of your teen's seizures changes, consult with your pediatric neurologist. He may wish to make medication changes.

DEALING WITH OTHER CHANGES

Most new issues you will face when your teen reaches puberty are the same ones that any parent of a teen faces, but they can be harder to deal with if your child has autism. Acne is often an indicator of the hormonal changes in puberty, and you may have difficulties getting your child to care for her skin. Establish a routine that keeps your teen's skin clean and free of oil and bacteria; cleansing pads are good for this purpose. An appointment with a dermatologist may also be helpful.

If you haven't seen the reality of "growing pains," you may become aware of them now. If your child seems irritable or tends to absently rub her arms and legs, be suspicious that literal growing pains may be the problem. Plenty of calcium is important at this stage in a teen's life, so if your child does not drink milk, ask your teen's physician about calcium supplements.

Other physical changes are normal and natural but may confuse your teenager. Body hair begins to appear, boys' voices crack, girls develop breasts—your teen wakes up in a new and unfamiliar body.

Emotional Changes of Puberty

Even more dramatic than the physical changes are the emotional and mental changes that a teenager experiences as she abandons childhood for adolescence. Autism is isolating and puberty can complicate the situation.

It is the parents' job to make certain that their teenagers continue to do the things they are capable of doing for themselves. It is true that a teenager with autism may not be interested in the latest fashions the kids are wearing at her school, but Mom and Dad need to be sure that she chooses appropriate clothing. Your teenager may not care about the latest haircut or even whether she has taken a shower, but you need to emphasize the importance of cleanliness and good grooming. A teenager's world turns on social acceptance, and since kids with autism struggle with social interaction, they will need all of the help they can get at this age.

Other emotional changes can include fragile feelings, willfulness, belligerence—your teenager may experience the complete range of emotions any adolescent has on entering puberty. If your teen is inclined toward aggression or anger outbursts, do not be surprised if the nature of those outbursts increase in frequency and severity.

Sexuality

It is difficult for parents when any child grows from the relative innocence of childhood to adulthood; sexuality is a topic that requires education, explanation, and understanding. It can be bewildering and even frightening for a child. But when the child has autism, the problem is magnified. How does a person with autism express her sexuality when her social skills are challenged?

MOM AND DAD, YOU NEED TO TALK

The two of you will need to sit down together and discuss how you feel about explaining puberty, adolescence, sexuality, and the role of sexuality to your children. It is important that you agree on issues of such importance. Individuals with autism will have unique as well as diverse problems with sexuality. The only common thread all those on the autism spectrum have is that their problems with socialization affect their behavior.

Many adults are uncomfortable about dealing with the sexuality of their children. Your mindfulness techniques can help you detach from your feelings on this subject so that you can have a dialogue about it with your child. If the conversation is delayed, you will find yourself facing an even more uncomfortable conversation after a bad situation arises.

Some people with autism do not have a sexual drive, and if that is the case, there is no reason to try to change this. Some medications can cause a loss of libido; other times the cause is unknown. Given the problems that a person with autism might encounter with sexuality, a lack of sexual drive could be a blessing in disguise.

UNDERSTANDING SEXUALITY

A person with autism who has a functioning libido will have difficulties expressing her sexuality in an appropriate manner. Matters of disease prevention, sexual abuse, birth control, and behavior management are difficult to explain to a young person, or an adult, who struggles with understanding concepts. As with the other things in your child's life that you have had to control, if the autism is severe enough to limit judgment, you need to take control of the sexuality as well. If it is any consolation, it will be harder on you as a parent than it will be on your child. No one wants to deny their child a life full of love and experiences, but sometimes it is the only choice available.

"Informed consent" between two adults is the generally accepted measure of whether a sexual activity is appropriate. Understanding what informed consent is will help you as a parent to assist your child as she grows up. There can be no informed consent unless each individual can:

○ Understand and communicate to another person the word or the meaning of the word "no."

○ If given different choices, demonstrate the ability to make a choice based on available information.

○ Understand that there are appropriate places and times for sexual behavior.

○ Understand and detect danger and threats in order to react properly.

○ Understand the word "no" and be able to cease an activity if told to do so.

There are many more factors involved in determining a person's ability to make an informed choice, but if a teenager lacks these skills, she is not capable of making sexual decisions for herself. And even if a teen communicates well and clearly, social interactions may still be beyond her grasp. Saying "no" does a person little good if she doesn't know when to say it.

It is wise when working on an IEP with school personnel to include these issues. It is important that they know you are aware of potential problems with your teen's sexuality. It is also helpful for the teachers and aides to work on helping your child to understand when saying "no" is appropriate.

UNWANTED SEXUAL ADVANCES

Parents need to consider the risk factors as they make decisions regarding their child's sexuality. HIV/AIDS is a risk with any kind of unprotected sexual contact involving body fluids. Children with autism are also easy targets for sexual abuse, as they do not always understand dangerous, threatening, or inappropriate situations.

Children and adults with autism have every right to friendships and relationships. If parents are in charge of their child's sexuality, their goal should be to help the child understand sexuality as much as possible to prevent the child from becoming a victim of unwanted sexual activity. When a child has a sexual experience against her will, or without her understanding, it is very hard on the entire family.

Menstruation

Considering what a frightening thing the onset of menstruation can be for a girl, it can be much more so if there are communication deficits. It may be natural, but it is still blood, and it can be alarming. The transition for girls with autism can be difficult, but it can be done. All that's required is sensitivity and some education.

INDICATIONS OF MENARCHE

The best way to help a girl beginning her menstrual cycle is to be prepared ahead of time. Watching for the signs that show your daughter is entering into menarche will allow you to teach her as much as possible about what is happening to her body and prepare her for what is to come.

When girls enter puberty, one of the first indications may be their behavior. Parents will notice irritability, which will be difficult to distinguish from the irritability or angry outbursts associated with autism. It takes little to provoke a bad mood and anger outbursts in a pubescent girl. Things that were once loved are now a source of embarrassment. But how do you recognize the arrival of puberty in a child when irritability and outbursts have always been part of the daily routine?

One helpful aspect of the menstrual cycle is that it can often be charted, although beginning menstrual periods may be quite irregular. People with autism often like to use a calendar, loving the structure of the routine, and if a girl's cycle is regular this can help parents plan.

It is important for the parents of a girl with autism to be attuned to their daughter's behavior. Routines can now be your best friend—even though you may have felt a slave to them in the past, they can help you be aware of what is going on with your daughter. If you notice that things are upsetting her that didn't six or twelve months ago, and you see a hair-trigger temper, that is a warning sign.

Breast development is usually the first physical sign that puberty has started. Her figure will start changing and she will develop hips and a waistline. She may develop quickly or slowly, as each girl's growth pattern is different. These are changes she may or may not acknowledge depending on how aware she is of her own body. At this point, it is time to start preparing her for the onset of her menses.

PREPARING YOUR DAUGHTER

Purchase supplies and select several different brands for your daughter to see. She may have a sensory reaction to one product and prefer another one based on criteria that aren't obvious to you. The color of the package, the shape of the pad, or an odor associated with the packaging will be some of her determining variables.

When you begin teaching your daughter how to handle the hygiene issues of having a period, it is important that a woman be part of the instructional process through discussions and use of diagrams. If you are a single dad, you need to find some help. A girl should never believe that it is appropriate and acceptable for anyone, male or female, of any age or relationship to her, to be in any kind of intimate contact with her. That is a rule that must never be broken. Single fathers can rely on their own mother, sister, a school nurse, or another trusted female. It is impossible to teach a girl what is appropriate for her own body if that rule is not adhered to closely.

Buy an easy-to-read calendar and put it in the bathroom. Begin by showing your daughter the calendar and the pads you purchased. Talk to her as though she understands each word you say even if she is totally nonverbal.

If the menstrual cycle is extremely difficult and hygiene is a constant battle, discuss your options with your daughter's doctor. Some physicians put girls with autism on medication or give an injection to suppress their periods. This may be an option for your child if it is medically appropriate.

When the big day arrives—and remember, you will have no warning of the actual date—fall back on your planning techniques. Take it in stride as you circle the day on the calendar and attend to clean up and hygiene matters. Remember to teach her proper disposal of the pads, and be sure you have a supply of her preferred brand.

Remember, children with autism do best with routine and clear expectations. If there are any hiccups, use your mindfulness strategies to convey calmness; the chances are much greater she will take it in stride.

Birth Control

It is easier for parents to make decisions regarding their child's sexuality if they proceed thoughtfully and cautiously. Sexuality is always a matter of informed consent between two adults. Factoring in the mental age of your child and her social abilities is essential. Unfortunately, no policy can exclude the possibility of sexual conduct that is unplanned, and for girls on the autism spectrum, this is a problem.

Most states do not allow permanent methods of birth control to be used on children, even if they are over the age of majority. There are no exceptions to those laws for children with disabilities. If your child is impaired enough that having children is out of the question, check with a gynecologist and the laws in your state to find out what can and cannot be done.

So how do parents prevent an unplanned pregnancy that is the result of their child engaging in sexual contact without understanding the implications of the activity? Many physicians will prescribe a birth control method for girls with autism or other spectrum disorders that can be taken daily in a pill form, injected every few weeks (frequency depending on the patient), or implanted. The advantage to the injections or implants is that the concern is removed without the daily use of a pill. The disadvantage can be the possible side effects of these methods of birth control, including weight gain, headaches, and problems that may be associated with long-term use of these medications.

Inappropriate Behaviors

Although there are many behaviors that can be considered inappropriate, none upset people quite like those behaviors that are sexual in nature. Children become aware at very young ages that it is inappropriate to touch other people in certain places; children with autism can be taught this also. It is important to deal with these behaviors when a child is young so that they are not a problem when he or she becomes an adult.

SELF-STIMULATING BEHAVIORS
This is a sensitive subject for all parents when they discover their child masturbating without any discretion and they wonder how to handle the situation. To keep a proper perspective, remember that almost all children masturbate. Children with autism have no inhibitions, because they are unaware of the social taboo against masturbating in public. It is your job to guide them at an early age to prevent long-term problems.

POSSIBLE CAUSES OF EXCESSIVE TOUCHING IN CHILDREN
Not all touching by children is sexually driven. There could be a variety of reasons they are touching themselves.

O Underwear may be too tight and be causing chafing.

O She may be reacting to the laundry detergent.

- He may have pinworms.

- She may have vaginal discharge.

- He may not have fully cleaned himself after toileting.

Many parents are embarrassed when they see their child touching herself, particularly in public. There are ways you can teach children from an early age not to inappropriately or publicly touch themselves. This will carry into adolescence and adulthood, but the parent must teach the child through the use of a routine on how to care for herself that she can adhere to that will prevent further problems.

When you clearly model and teach your children appropriate boundaries, chances are better that they will not do things in public that will embarrass you.

- Make sure you are always properly dressed.

- Monitor what your children are seeing. Do not allow them to see inappropriate scenes on television that they will imitate.

- Provide undergarments that fit correctly and are made of a soft material.

- Teach them how to properly clean themselves. From a young age, teach them how to wash themselves and instruct them that their privates are for washing. Because children with autism understand routine and rules, tell them that this area is to be cleaned, that this is what they should be doing with this area, and they will incorporate this into their daily routine. By teaching them to clean themselves, you are also teaching them how to soothe and take care of themselves.

If you do find your child inappropriately touching himself, please tell him to stop but do not holler or scream. Simply instruct him to take his hands out of his pants and change his focus by redirecting him to another activity. If you become upset, he will become upset and have a hard time being redirected.

INAPPROPRIATE TOUCHING OF OTHERS

The majority of paraprofessionals that work with students with autism are female. Women are also still in a majority as caregivers, whether it be at home, daycare, or in other environments that care for children. A young boy with autism may try touching one of these women in a sexual manner that is not acceptable. Do not be surprised if you find out that your son has tried this.

If he has not been taught at a young age to not touch others, he will probably attempt to do this. The behavior must be stopped. You do not want to ignore this behavior in small children; if it's allowed to continue, it is extremely difficult to stop when he becomes an adolescent and there can be severe consequences for him when he is a thirty-year-old man. The most important thing that parents and school personnel can do is teach that inappropriate touching of others is not allowed in any circumstance.

Staying Sensitive to Your Child's Changes

As your children mature, you will want to remember that they are now becoming a young man and a young woman regardless of whether they have a disability. It can be challenging for parents to let go and allow their children to grow up. However, doing so is vital to help them become independent and contribute to society. Things to keep in mind will be to:

- Guide and teach them age-appropriate skills.

- Refrain from teasing or making fun of them.

- Have pictures of them from when they were little and show them how they are growing up so they can understand the changes they are experiencing.

- Get them involved in age-appropriate activities as they mature, such as the Special Olympics, arts and crafts, bowling, tennis, reading, writing, and bike riding.

- Teach them life skills that are really meaningful.

○ Discover what will help them grow so they can continue to progress toward the next level of life skills.

○ Continue to check on them, but you will not need the level of monitoring and instruction that you provided when they were small.

○ Continue to attend support groups to educate yourself on how others are teaching age-appropriate skills and dealing with sensitive situations.

Important Points to Consider

The teenage years can be fun for adolescents with autism, and their parents, once they all know how to navigate some of the trickier issues of puberty!

○ You can be respectful of your child's changes by teaching her meaningful age-appropriate skills and encouraging her to participate in fun activities.

○ Support groups can help you learn how to deal with sensitive situations.

○ A child with autism must be taught when young that he cannot touch others inappropriately. If this behavior is allowed, it will be extremely difficult to stop when he becomes an adolescent or adult.

○ You can prepare and teach your daughter how to deal with menstruation by creating a structure and schedule.

○ You can check on your adolescent to make sure he is grooming; however, you will not need to monitor him as you did when he was young.

CHAPTER 14

Autism and Life As an Adult

When people start a family, they have expectations and goals for their children; one of those goals is having their children become independent. Most parents want their adult children to be able to feel equipped to move successfully in the world. Having a child with autism may require parents to reassess this goal and determine what can be an appropriate future for their child. As your child approaches adulthood, you will have many opportunities to understand his unique gifts and challenges. The transition to adulthood can be challenging for parents, as they have to let go of how they've seen their child and help him become even more independent. Also, determining whether their child is capable of living independently or in a group setting or should stay at home with the family are big decisions. Using your mindfulness practice can help you begin to slowly and calmly explore all of your options.

Living Independently

In a perfect world, children with autism would mature and acquire the skills they need to live on their own. They would understand the things that are needed to live safely: turning off stoves, locking doors, and handling all the daily activities about which most people never give a second thought.

Coping depends on the ability to understand what is needed in a particular situation and being able to perform or think through what steps need to be taken. If a young person has impaired judgment, he might not be able to handle living independently.

ACTIVITIES OF DAILY LIVING (ADL)

An important part of determining whether your adult child can live independently is to be sure that he can be fully responsible for his own personal care and hygiene. This means that he can independently:

O Bathe or shower daily

O Use the bathroom

O Use deodorant, skin care products, and other toiletries appropriately

O Brush and floss his teeth

O Brush his hair

O Dress properly for weather conditions

O Dress appropriately for work, leisure, and sleep

O Determine which clothes need to be laundered

O Take medications at the proper times in the proper dosages

Many people with autism learn how to do all of these things and develop a routine they faithfully maintain. If you have a child who is ten years old and has not mastered some of these skills, don't worry. Remember, children with autism are whizzes at routine, so the more structured a routine you offer, the more comfortable he will be when he has his own system to care for himself. Parents sometimes forget that children who do not have autism resist brushing their teeth and washing their hands, so failure to do so isn't always autism—sometimes it is just being a kid!

Building the Daily Care Habits

As parents work with a child to build the habits and skills he will need as an adult, the need for routine will work in his favor. For those who respond well to video, there is an app available on iTunes (*www.apple.com/itunes*) called Pictello. Pictello allows you to create a customized video of your child doing any task. It can include the pictures of him doing the task, along with written or verbal language to reinforce what he is doing. He can replay the video every time he needs instructions to complete a task. It is an amazing way to create independence for any kind of self-care, work, or educational task.

MAKING LISTS

Before you begin building a routine to teach activities of daily living, sit down with a piece of paper and pencil and outline all of the skills that are necessary for your child. All people have some common activities, such as bathing or showering and using the toilet, but there are many individual ones as well. For example, some children need to use certain skin care products to treat acne or eczema.

Make a list and divide it into three parts: morning, afternoon, and evening. In your three-part schedule, list the activities that occur, or should occur, during those times. For instance, the morning list might include using the toilet, brushing teeth, showering, taking medications, and so forth. Make this list for each of the three parts of the day in your child's schedule, itemizing all the activities you can think of. Keep the list handy for a few days and add in the things you overlooked so the list will be as complete as possible.

CREATING A COMMUNICATION BOARD

If your child is nonverbal, make a communication board and put it in the bathroom where he will be able to reference it easily; above a sink is a good location for something of this nature. You can attach small drawings that represent the activity or you can use photographs. Attach them with Velcro so you can adjust the order in which things are done if necessary.

An instant camera can make quick work of creating visual cues to help your child understand his life and routine. Take photos of him brushing his teeth, bathing, eating, etc., and of his clothes and other items he uses. This will make your communication board unique and specific to his needs.

Join your child daily in performing the morning routine. Make it fun for him to do it with you. In simple language, as you go through the activities, explain to him what he is to do and point to the picture on the communication board. If he can understand what he reads, another option is to have a chart on the wall where he can read the activities he needs to complete. After three to four weeks, he will have developed a new routine. Keep an eye on it until you are confident he has mastered the skills. As he becomes independent, you'll step away from overseeing each step and simply check on him to make sure he is doing okay.

Repeat this entire procedure for the afternoon and evening care. The most important part is that both you and your child follow the schedule consistently.

Residential Living

Some parents have their child with autism live at home after reaching adulthood. However, this is not always the best choice for an adult child or for the parents. There are other available options and there is no single, best solution for a given child. It isn't just the child's abilities that determine what is best for the family. It is also the family's needs, lifestyle, available emotional and physical resources, and finances.

REMAINING AT HOME

This is one of the most frequently discussed topics in support groups across the country. Someone will usually, and tentatively, ask the question "What do I do when my child is grown?" The most important consideration in deciding where your child will live as an adult should be whether the environment is productive and interesting. Whether your child lives at home with you, in a group home, or in a setting providing full-time care, you want to provide an environment that can bring him as much happiness and satisfaction as possible.

The tendency for isolation makes it imperative that the family be able to provide the adult with autism opportunities for meaningful engagement. He will need to participate in various activities, have a schedule that keeps him interested, stick to the schedule as much as possible, and be physically active. You will need to either keep up with that schedule yourself or have someone in the home who can. You will also need to plan ahead to make arrangements for someone to care for your child when age and health make it impossible for you to do so.

GROUP HOMES

Group homes and assisted living are the options most parents choose for their children on the autism spectrum. Group homes generally have four to six residents. Two staff members are on the schedule at all times except during sleeping hours, when one is sufficient, and other personnel for special therapies come in and out. These homes are usually single-family residences in neighborhoods around the country. Activities are planned regularly, such as swimming, bowling, and field trips. Group homes can teach young adults the skills necessary to live independently or return home to live with parents and other family members.

Assisted living is for people with high-functioning autism who need less supervision than those in a group home. Two people may share living arrangements and have a social services worker visit daily to be sure that their needs are being met. Each of these situations would vary depending on the people involved and their abilities.

LONG-TERM CARE

Some people with autism need round-the-clock care and supervision. There are long-term care facilities that are both modern and comfortable. They are clean without looking like a hospital, are geared toward meeting the needs of the residents, and are staffed by professionals who enjoy working with those with severe needs.

A long-term care facility may be appropriate for a person with autism who has severe behaviors that can be a source of danger to him or others or who requires a great deal of therapy or monitoring. Group homes or assisted living facilities do not provide this level of intensive supervision.

Whether a parent chooses a long-term care facility, group home, or assisted living facility, or keeps an adult child with autism at home, it is an individual choice. If you are having problems making these decisions, use your mindfulness practices and/or seek professional advice so that you can make the most effective choices for your family.

Providing after You Are Gone

One of the biggest concerns you may face as a parent is how to provide for your special-needs child after you are gone. Having a will is an important part of determining how your child will be cared for. There are attorneys who specialize in creating special-needs trusts who will advise you how you can correctly provide for your child.

ASSET PROTECTION

When a young couple marries and begins to build a life, they usually make plans for the future. Very seldom do they think that the decisions they make in their twenties may affect their baby when he is a senior citizen. But it is important for parents of a child with autism to protect all of their assets to provide for their child when he is an adult.

If you name someone in your will to care for your child's finances, be absolutely certain of your confidence and trust in this person. It might be wise to consider a certified accountant to protect your child's interests. You also need to be sure that the individual you name knows of and has agreed to your decision in advance.

TRUST FUNDS

A parent often sets up a trust fund to provide for a child's needs. Because a child with autism is not likely to understand money management when he is an adult, preparations to protect his future are important. Although a will does declare where you wish your assets to go, a trust fund has funds and assets that can be distributed over a person's lifetime. As with guardianship, it is important to select a trusted friend or organization to oversee the trust fund. It is possible to select more than one trustee if you wish to have the responsibility shared.

Each state has different laws governing how trusts are set up and maintained, and it is important that you are aware of your state's regulations. Most states have two types of trust funds, one of which is of particular interest to the parents of a child who has special needs. An after-death trust is set up to protect the financial needs of a child when both parents are deceased. An estate attorney can best advise you concerning your specific needs, concerns, and state laws.

Although many states have made it legal for you to write your own will, this is not wise if your child has a disability. If a parent has made her own will, it is more vulnerable to being successfully contested. It would be wise to get the assistance of a lawyer who specializes in special needs.

The trustee or person you appoint to oversee the trust must be someone you trust implicitly. Trustees are held to a high accountability, both legally and morally, and they may be paid a fee for their services, as the judgment they provide is invaluable. If you choose a family member or friend, be certain she understands financial management. If she can be trusted to fulfill your wishes and your child's needs but lacks some knowledge in the finer points of money management, don't hesitate to also appoint an accountant or other professional to advise your primary trustee and realize that this professional person will bill the trust for his or her services whenever rendered, unless a lump-sum fee was agreed upon at the time of appointment.

Guardians

If something happens to you or your spouse, do you know who will take care of your children—especially your child with autism? Most people feel confident that a family member would step in, but when a crisis such as this happens, it doesn't always work out that smoothly. It may be impossible for grandparents, due to age or health, to assume the responsibility for your child. It may also be more than another family member can handle if he is raising a family already. Do not assume anything.

A SERIOUS DISCUSSION

In choosing potential guardians, make a list of the people you feel would be best able to raise your special-needs child in the event you are unable to do so. Then talk to those people in a setting where you have their total attention. This is a serious decision for all parties concerned, and not an "off the cuff" conversation. Outline what your child's needs are now and what those needs are apt to be in the future. Explain what financial resources would be available, what health issues your child has, and what your expectations are for his future.

As you compile this list of people, think about your child, his life, and the lives of the people you are considering asking. If it is a family member, perhaps your own sister, does she have a career that might make this responsibility difficult? A career military officer, for example, may be stationed anywhere in the world or called to active service with little advance notice, and she would then have the same problem of deciding who would step in. Also, consider the person's lifestyle and how she feels about her family life. One person who has eight children might easily handle another one, even one with autism, but another person with a large family might panic at the idea of another child.

> You may hope your other children would step in to care for their brother with autism if the need arose. But the truth is that siblings may not feel up to taking on such a challenge. It can also place an unfair burden on a sibling. If a sibling is named as a caretaker in your will, she should have agreed in advance to be designated, and should be listed in addition to alternate individuals.

When you approach a person about assuming care of your child, he may have several reactions. It's possible that he would want to, or insist on, caring for your child. Alternatively, he might like to think it through and consider different options. Or he may realize immediately that this would not be the right decision for him or his family. There is no right or wrong answer to this request.

A CONTROVERSIAL CHOICE

Sometimes parents make decisions about guardianship that are not understood by family members, and can cause conflict. It would be so easy to say that the only way to avoid a problem is not to tell anyone, reasoning that a conflict probably won't arise and if one does, you won't have to hear about it anyway. Consider, though, the people you have chosen. If your family members do not know in advance what your wishes are, and yet you have made those choices official in your will, bad feelings could result, and a custody battle could ensue.

You may revise your choice of a guardian every few years. Your child's needs will change over time and you will understand them better as he matures. Other people's lives change as well. Plan ahead and be flexible to change when it is necessary.

It may be because of a lack of closeness with other family members, or you may know about financial or other circumstances that would limit your relatives' ability to accept this challenge. Whatever your reason, should you choose a non-relative to care for your child in the event of your death, do not feel guilty or pressured to change your arrangements. You and your spouse—or if you are single, you alone—know what is best.

When you are writing your will, you may also want to draw up a living will. This document states your wishes about what you want done for your own care in case of a serious hospitalization or accident. You also may consider having a lawyer draw up a document for your health care power of attorney, which gives legal power to others to act for you if you are temporarily or permanently incapacitated.

When you have a list of people who would be willing to act as guardian, state those people by name in your will as your choices to raise your children. It is wise to have several names in case something prevents one of them from stepping in. If you have more than one name on the list in your will, you can avoid having to rewrite it every six months or so, and it will save attorney's fees. It will also give you peace of mind to know that you have done all you can to protect your child and his interests.

Financial Protection

Every family attempts to protect itself financially, but when there is a child with autism involved, this protection becomes much more critical. Mom and Dad find they are making decisions that affect the distant future as well as the here and now.

INSURANCE

When you are young, you think you will live forever. Everyone realizes her own mortality at a different age, but it doesn't usually happen when a person is in her twenties. However, that is the time when life insurance is less expensive, and easy to acquire.

A staggering number of parents find themselves widowed with small children, and out of those, a large number of them have no life insurance to fall back on. Imagine a woman who has been staying at home with the kids for years unexpectedly losing her husband; without insurance, she may have no financial resources available. Social Security will pick up the burden for a period of time in such cases. You may qualify for Supplemental Security Income (SSI) or another form of state aid, but these are not long-term solutions.

IRAS AND OTHER FUNDS

Parents can, through their employer, set up various financial plans that should protect and increase their money over the years. IRAs and other retirement plans may be able to protect a family in different ways. Tax benefits can be seen immediately, and funds will be available to provide for family members upon retirement or in the case of an unexpected death. IRAs supersede the will, so be certain you keep your beneficiary or beneficiaries updated.

Every state differs in regulations regarding financial matters. Financial planning is a complex subject with many pitfalls for the uninformed. If you are planning to set up a portfolio for your family's security, consult with an accountant and estate-planning attorney for the best course of action. You will be preparing not just for your lifetime, but for your child's lifetime as well.

Important Points to Consider

Having a child with autism may require parents to reassess their goals and determine what can be an appropriate future for their child.

O In order for your child to live independently as an adult, you will want to make sure that he can take care of all of his own self-care needs.

O There are living options for adulthood. Some parents keep their children home with them; other children live in group homes or assisted living facilities, or require extensive monitoring in a long-term care facility.

O Guardianship is an important issue that will need special consideration and time to decide.

O Having a will that includes a special-needs trust will make sure you provide for your child when you are no longer available to care for him.

CHAPTER 15

Challenging Obstacles with an Engaged Presence

When a person has an engaged presence, he is able to give undivided attention to the person he is communicating with. As a parent, being engaged and present with your child will help your relationship in many ways. It will allow you to deepen your bond with your child by being aware of and responsive to the subtle signals that your child is communicating. You enter into engaged presence each time you apply your mindfulness practice of slowing down, breathing, and becoming aware of your own inner responses before reacting. In the following sections, you'll learn ways you can handle challenging situations with engaged presence in order to have more peace in your household.

Conscious Parenting Triggers

Triggers are thoughts or feelings that you experience that are based on events that have occurred in the past. Triggers can be positive or negative. Triggers, from a negative vantage point, interfere with your ability to know how to help your child, particularly one who has significant difficulties with communication. These feelings can make you "freeze" and feel more helpless, which prevents you from being able to correctly discern and problem solve. These triggers can cause you to:

O Not know what to do to meet your child's needs

O Not understand what your child's behavior is telling you

O Think that in order to meet your child's needs you have to be able to read her mind

O Think you are an inadequate or bad parent

O Feel overwhelmed by the amount of challenges you are managing

O Feel guilty

O Forget how you successfully handled something in the past

O Worry that you cannot read your child's signs, cues, and behaviors and actually miss what she is communicating

If you have been triggered, you may find it shows up in your responses, reactions, and behaviors. Have you ever noticed that if you have not had enough sleep or are worried, you find yourself yelling at your children, or fighting with your spouse or relatives? When you are triggered you could find yourself having difficulties allowing yourself to rest, relax, or simply enjoy yourself.

Communicating Needs

One of the biggest triggers for any parent is feeling ill equipped to meet your child's needs. This becomes heightened when the child has difficulties communicating. Because children with autism have trouble expressing their needs in a way you can understand, parents have to develop other ways to tune into and read the child. This can be done; however, if a parent is very upset or anxious, it becomes much more difficult. Mindfulness practices can help. When you feel worried or worked up because you cannot figure out what your child is trying to communicate to you, try slowing down and taking a few breaths. Your child will notice this and will calm down in response to the shift in your energy.

WAYS TO LEARN TO ANTICIPATE YOUR CHILD'S NEEDS

In the early days, you will have to learn to anticipate what your child needs. Some parents are so focused on their frustration and on wishing their child had language that they miss the cues their child is sending them. Learning to anticipate your child's needs will require you to really slow down and relax. It does not happen when you are busy, frantic, or caught in chaos. You'll simply be too distracted to pay attention to what she is attempting to communicate, and she will feel your angst and retreat even more. Believe it or not, children with autism will try to communicate what they want, and if they feel that you care and are patient with them, they will also continue to communicate with you until you get it. Using a communication board or system will help a lot, as your child will have a place to begin to communicate with you.

When a child is unable to communicate her needs, know that she is just as frustrated as you are. Try taking a step back for a moment by breathing deeply and slowing yourself down. Let her know that you genuinely want to understand her. You may be surprised what she begins to eventually share with you as she feels your love.

Learning How to Handle Challenging Situations

Over time you will develop skills to know how to manage difficult situations. The following sections will introduce you to basic principles about these challenging situations and ways that you can handle them by using mindfulness.

ILLNESS

"I couldn't believe it. I didn't get him to the doctor for two days. I didn't even know he was sick." A mother spoke with all the guilt she was feeling. "I should have known. I don't think I am a very good mom." This mom didn't realize that there was no way she could have known her child was ill. Contrary to what children think, parents do not have eyes in the back of their head and are not able to read minds.

Some symptoms are obvious. A child who is vomiting is clearly ill and needs attention. You won't know exactly what the child feels, but you will see that she is sick and needs immediate treatment. Likewise, a rash can be seen and treated. These are objective symptoms, which means they can be measured, seen, heard, or felt by another person.

A subjective symptom, on the other hand, is a symptom that the child feels but that is not obvious to others, such as a headache.

You will have little trouble spotting the objective symptoms, and as time passes, you will get better and better at this. You will develop a sixth sense that will alert you that your child is ill—long before a parent of a child without autism might notice the same illness. The clues are subtle but you will learn to notice them and know there is a problem to be handled.

Most children become cranky when they are ill and this is intensified if the child has autism.

Subjective symptoms are another matter entirely and create particular problems for parents with children who have communication difficulties.

For a child who is not on the autism spectrum, the subjective feelings of illness are often what prevent him from getting sicker, because he can tell his parents how he is feeling and they can then start appropriate treatment at home or with a physician. A child without autism will come home from school and announce he has a headache and feels rotten. Mom or Dad will feel his forehead, put him to bed to be on the safe side, and take preventative measures to keep him from becoming sicker. It isn't that simple for your child with autism. She will come home from school with the same headache, feeling just as miserable, and you may not have a clue.

This is where guilt comes in. Big-time guilt! The next morning your child awakens with a fever and rash, is very lethargic, and has glassy eyes, and you nominate yourself for the Worst Parent in the World award. Then it's off to the doctor and you come back home with the frustrating diagnosis of "It's a virus," and everyone moves on. Know that you are not the worst parent in the world, despite how you may feel at that moment.

IS MY CHILD SICK?

It is very difficult to determine if a child with autism is ill unless the objective symptoms jump out and announce themselves. Knowing indicators of illness can help you reflect and determine what is going on with your child.

O *Watch for alterations in your child's routine.* You know that your child has a routine and you are quite familiar with it; your whole life is scheduled according to that routine. When it changes abruptly for no apparent reason, that is a red flag that something is wrong and it is time to investigate the possibility your child is getting sick.

O *Watch for changes in behaviors.* For example, a child may line up objects around the house and you expect this. It may be more prevalent on one day than another, but it is something you know will happen. But if suddenly everything in your house is lined up and your child becomes very aggressive about keeping her lines in order, this is a new manifestation of a previously observed behavior.

○ *Look at the changes in her activity levels.* A child who suddenly curls up on the sofa, covers herself with a blanket, and stares at the television is probably not up to snuff. How does your child react to her siblings or pets? Are her actions typical or does she refuse to interact in her normal manner? If your child would never turn down a tussle with a brother but today she ignores his baiting, she may be sick.

○ *Consider how she is responding to touch.* If your child tends to reject physical closeness as a rule but suddenly shows a desire to be hugged and cuddled, feel her forehead while you are getting that snuggle—you may find that she has a fever.

○ *Are her eating habits different?* When a child with autism rejects her favorite foods, look for symptoms of an illness.

○ *Look for changes in her appearance and responses.* Do her eyes look flat or glassy? Does she rub her tummy or try to lie down? Use your instincts as a parent and check for a hot forehead or signs of a cold.

If you find you have a hard time trusting your instincts, use your mindfulness practice to take three breaths and slow down. This will help you develop your instincts to calmly problem solve more instead of simply reacting.

As you and your child learn more and more about each other, you will be surprised at how quickly you will tune into her when she isn't feeling well, and how over time you will know how to correctly respond to meet her needs.

Safety Concerns

Most safety issues you'll have with your child are the same ones all parents have with young children. However, these issues will be amplified because of the autistic tendency to disregard danger, resulting from poor impulse control.

Below are some of the more important safety hazards within the home:

○ Stoves, refrigerators, microwave ovens, and irons are items that intrigue children and can cause serious injury.

○ Electrical appliances (hair dryers, curling irons, shavers, etc.) in the bathroom are accidents waiting to happen.

○ Water and a young child with autism are a dangerous combination. Be sure your child eventually learns to swim, but keep in mind how hazardous a bathtub can be. Also check the temperature of your hot water. A child can be badly scalded if the water is too hot. The hot water heater should be turned down below a temperature of 120°F.

○ The family medications should be in a box that can be locked with a key, to prevent a curious child who is oral from harming herself.

○ Keep mirrors or glass doors out of your child's bedroom, and if she begins a tantrum near glass, remove her immediately to a safer location.

○ Electrical outlets are something "open" in the eyes of a child with compulsive tendencies; if she attempts to plug something into the outlet, she could be seriously injured. Special covers that are hard to remove can be purchased for outlets.

○ Keep scissors, knives, and any other sharp objects out of reach.

○ Washing machines and dryers can be hazardous for young children and for their pets. Cats do not enjoy the spin cycle—and, yes, it does happen.

Teach your child the picture symbol, sign, or word for "help." Be sure everyone she is regularly in contact with also knows the sign so they can respond to her. This can make all the difference in the world in preventing serious trouble.

Toilet Training

You can toilet train a child with autism by making it into a routine, which is the most effective system to help these children develop habits. This process has to be done consistently through guidance by the parent, and eventually the child can become responsible for going to the bathroom independently. Anytime she finishes consuming liquid or food, you will guide her to the bathroom so she links drinking and eating with going to the bathroom.

A powerful toilet training routine looks like this:

1. Upon waking up in the morning, the parent takes the child to the bathroom and the child uses the toilet.

2. After the child eats breakfast, she goes to the bathroom.

3. If the child has to take medications, the parent guides her to the bathroom.

4. If she has a morning snack, she goes to the bathroom.

5. She enjoys her lunch, then she goes to the bathroom.

6. After her afternoon snack, she goes directly to the bathroom.

7. Upon completion of dinner, she goes to the bathroom.

8. She uses the toilet before going to bed.

Here's the interesting part of how you can make toilet training successful. You actually make it a thrill to go to the bathroom, no matter what you are doing in there! Speak to your child as if it is the most exciting thing in the world: "Let's go to the potty! This will be so fun!" Share the moment with her and enjoy it.

Have the child use the regular toilet with a stepstool and an adaptive potty seat. Don't use a baby toilet. Children with autism want to be big girls and big boys just like their siblings. You have to make sure to treat them this way if you do not want them to continue to act like small children.

Create a positive bond and experience right there in the bathroom. Have a book or a toy that she can play with only in the bathroom. This will give her an incentive to go into the bathroom, and something she can look forward to. Create some joy and happiness that only happens in the bathroom.

After she uses the toilet, reward her with "Wow, good job!" and a smile, love, laughter, and a kiss. Let her know you are proud of her.

This is the way to create a calm toilet training experience, without tension, crying, or acting up. It will be easier and more comfortable for you, and your child will feel this.

In the early stages of toilet training, you will want to be with your child in the bathroom. After awhile she will indicate to you that she can go on her own. Your job will be to simply monitor her by peeking your head in and asking, "How are you doing? Good job!" She will let you know when you don't need to check on her anymore. She will literally push you out of the bathroom, letting you know she's got it handled!

THE POWER OF VISUALIZATION

Using visual clues can be helpful in toilet training your child. When you communicate the desired behavior and she understands it, she will naturally be compliant. It is essential that the sequence of activities is clear and understood by your child.

A small communication board is very useful to teach the toileting process.

If you are following the system where you take her to the toilet after ingesting food or liquid as stated earlier in this chapter, you can initially use the "first, then" system to indicate what she will be doing. For instance, "first" she will eat and "then" she will be using the bathroom. This system helps reduce anxiety and keep her focused because she will know what is presently expected of her and what is coming next.

Initially, your child may need the communication board to understand the process of toileting and keep her on track. Over time, this process will become instinctual and the board will not be necessary.

A sample board may include the following symbols:

○ Pull down pants

○ Pull down underwear

○ Sit on the toilet

○ Use toilet paper if appropriate

○ Place toilet paper in the toilet

○ Flush toilet

○ Pull up underwear

○ Pull up pants

○ Wash hands

○ Finished

○ Check schedule

Tailor the communication board to meet your child's and household's specific needs.

VISUAL CUES

Some children do not understand picture schedules but can recognize a visual prop. This object notifies your child of the next expected activity. Many people use an object such as a rubber duck to indicate the bathroom is the next stop. Your child can also use this cue when he is older by handing it to you to tell you that he needs to use the bathroom.

TOILETING CONSIDERATIONS

○ **Inaccurate aim.** This is something boys have a tendency to do and can be helped by using a target in the toilet. Floating something in the water that is safe for the plumbing, like an M&M, can give them something to aim for.

- **Have your children clean up after themselves.** Do not do this for them. Young children can use a wipe and clean, as long as you teach them and expect them to do so.

- **Flushing inappropriate items.** Do not ever let your child see you flush anything that doesn't belong there. You understand that the goldfish went to fish heaven; your child may not understand that the hamster shouldn't go as well.

Important Points to Consider

Being engaged and present with your child will help you deepen your bond. It will allow you to become aware of and responsive to the subtle signals that your child is communicating.

- You can learn to read the signs to determine if your nonverbal child is sick. Watch for alterations in her routine, as well as changes in behaviors and activity levels and how she is responding to touch. Notice any changes in her eating habits, appearance, and overall responses.

- There are significant safety concerns with children with autism because of their lack of impulse control.

- You can successfully toilet train a child with autism by making it into a routine. This process, when done consistently, allows the child to become independent in the bathroom.

**CHAPTER 16**

Expanding Abilities Through Intervention

Beginning early intervention is an important step that parents can take to help their child with autism. If various therapies and treatments can begin before the age of three, the development of a child with autism is greatly enhanced.

Who's Who among Physicians

Although everyone agrees that finding a good physician can make all the difference to a family with a child with special needs, they also agree that it is very difficult to find one who is familiar with autism. A smart doctor will admit if he isn't well informed on the topic and will refer you to a specialist, or he will make an effort to learn all he can to benefit his patients. Throughout your child's growing years, you will likely have contact with several different physicians.

THE PEDIATRICIAN

Pediatricians are specialists who provide the medical care of children. They see children from birth to age eighteen and beyond in certain circumstances. Pediatrics is a specialty of medicine, as children are not just miniature adults—their health needs and issues are different and must be treated differently from the way an adult would be treated. Pediatricians have many years of college and training: eight years of college and medical school, one year of pediatric internship, and two or more years in pediatric residency.

A good pediatrician will take the time to learn about your entire family. She will ask about your family life and history. She is not prying, but rather is attempting to understand the environment in which your child lives and how it affects his health and well-being.

Pediatricians who are good with children with autism are kind yet firm, can relate to and enjoy nonverbal children, and have a lot of patience. There are now pediatricians who specialize only in treating people on the autistic spectrum.

Many parents feel that a team is necessary to provide proper care of their child, and the pediatrician is one of the most valued members of that team. The pediatrician should feel much the same way—that she is a

Use your mindfulness techniques if you are not comfortable with either the pediatrician or the staff and if the office doesn't seem well run and is not clean and child-friendly. Allow yourself to slow down by taking three breaths so you can determine if it would be wise to look for a new physician. You may need to visit two or three pediatricians before you find just the right one.

member of a team that has been assembled to help your child. Selecting the right pediatrician, one with whom you feel comfortable, is important. Begin by speaking with family and friends and, of course, your support group; collect a list of names and organize yourself so that you find the best physician you can. Then make an initial appointment with the doctor you select to see how you and your child relate to the doctor and the office staff.

THE PEDIATRIC NEUROLOGIST

Neurology is the study of brain and nervous system disorders. Pediatric neurologists are specialized in both neurology and pediatrics and have training in both fields. They treat conditions from headaches to brain tumors. Some have a special interest in autism, but many do not.

A pediatric neurologist will not be the source of primary care for your child. In other words, don't call his office for a sore throat or rash. However, if your child has a coexisting condition such as a seizure disorder, you will be working closely with this physician for many years.

THE CHILD PSYCHIATRIST OR PSYCHOLOGIST

It is hard not to balk when you are advised to consult with a child psychiatrist or psychologist. To keep this in the proper light, remember that mental-health professionals do more than work with mental illness; they have a unique understanding of how neurological disorders affect behavior and how best to treat these challenges.

A psychiatrist is a physician who has had additional training studying the brain and the mind. She will have had twelve years of training. The psychiatrist can prescribe medications, whereas other experts in mental health cannot. A child psychiatrist may also be helpful as a family adjusts to the diagnosis of autism.

Clinical psychologists will have either a master's degree or doctorate. One of their most important roles is to perform the diagnostic testing for your child, and they will often work with an entire family to modify undesirable behaviors in a child with autism.

All professionals in the mental health fields have to complete a certain number of hours of professional education annually. Look for a child psychiatrist or psychologist with a special interest in autism. If the professional regularly deals with autism, she should be up-to-date on issues, which should result in better care for your child.

Selecting the Right Physician

The first thing to do is organize your list by geographical convenience; it matters little how good a particular physician may be if you can't get to her office. You don't need to be in your doctor's backyard, but in an emergency, it is nice to have a doctor a few minutes away. The physician may have more than one office if it is a large practice, in which case knowing what days the doctor is in is helpful. While you are mapping out locations, it is also helpful to make a note of what hours the office is open. Many offices will be open in the evening one night a week to accommodate working parents.

Next, decide if you prefer a male or female physician. It may not matter to you or you may feel more comfortable with a physician of the same sex as your child. If you would be more comfortable with a physician of a certain age, write that in too. Older doctors have more experience but younger doctors may be more open and innovative; it depends on the personality of the physician. If you are uncomfortable asking someone's age, ask how many years she has been in practice.

Then begin interviewing. Call the office to set up an appointment, which should be a free-of-charge visit; tell the receptionist that you would like to schedule a "get acquainted" visit as you are choosing a physician for your child. Note the attitude of the staff on the telephone—in the future, those will be the first people you speak with. They should be friendly, helpful, and professional.

Finding the right dentist is extremely important for a child in the autism spectrum. Because of the extreme sensitivity to noise and touch that many of the children have, it is crucial to have a dentist skilled in working with these kids. Many children's hospitals and university medical centers have dental programs for children with special needs.

The physician, when you meet her, should be open and interested in your questions. She should feel no discomfort at being quizzed about how she would handle your child's care and development. You may want a doctor with a gentle sense of humor but not a flippant attitude. Ask questions specific to your concerns about autism to determine the doctor's level of experience with and interest in ASD. She will likely have questions for you, too, and setting up this dialogue is important for the future of your working relationship.

The Importance of Qualified Therapists

Medical care may be only as good as the ancillary medical professionals that provide it. Your child will see different therapists more often than his physician and it is important they are qualified, knowledgeable, and interested in their fields. You should be able to tell if the therapists you are seeing care about their work; checking their qualifications is also easy.

AUDIOLOGISTS AND SPEECH THERAPISTS

Audiologists are the head of the team that diagnoses and handles hearing disorders. They may also diagnose and recommend treatment for many communication disorders, but this also can be the role of a speech therapist. When a child has autism, an audiologist is frequently the first professional to see the child, because the parents usually suspect hearing loss. Audiologists should have at least a master's degree.

Audiologists are trained to work with young children and non-verbal children. They will use several techniques to determine whether a child has a hearing disorder or a receptive language problem. Although they do not diagnose autism, they are important for ruling out a hearing impairment.

Speech therapists, or speech and language pathologists, work with people who have many varied kinds of hearing or communication problems. In an average day, a speech therapist works with people of all ages and may see a child with a lisp, an older person who has had a stroke, a nonverbal child with autism, and a person with a hearing impairment. A speech-language pathologist has a minimum of a master's degree in which she has studied communication disorders, diagnostic methods, age-specific disorders, anatomy and physiology as it pertains to voice and, sometimes, swallowing disorders. The final year of master's degree study must include a clinical practicum of up to 375 hours of practice supervised by a licensed and certified speech therapist.

As your child begins therapy, regardless of what method you decide on, you will likely interact with a speech therapist. Talk to the therapist about your concerns regarding language development and what you can do at home to reinforce the therapy. There will be many small things that you do on a day-to-day basis that will help your child progress.

PHYSICAL THERAPISTS

Whether or not your child sees a physical therapist (PT) will depend on his gross motor skills. Many children with autism do not have any deficits in this area and do not need physical therapy, but others have extensive issues. The goal of physical therapy is to improve motor functioning. Issues such as range of motion and flexibility are primary concerns that will be addressed by the therapist. PTs work to increase a patient's independence by increasing balance, coordination, and strength.

If your physician recommends a PT, you may find your first visit with him to be much like a doctor visit. PTs will analyze a patient's medical history, conduct an evaluation of their own, and recommend a course of treatment. They will develop an appropriate therapy plan, coordinate all forms of therapy, and instruct parents on home activities to enforce the treatment plan.

PTs are college educated, with a minimum of a master's degree. They will be certified and belong to a variety of organizations. Continuing education is also a requirement for licensure. As with any kind of therapist, a special interest in autism is helpful.

OCCUPATIONAL THERAPISTS

One of the most important professionals your child will see will be the occupational therapist (OT). This person will be pivotal in helping your child build skills or develop alternative strategies to compensate for skills that have yet to emerge and are necessary for functioning in everyday life. The OT may also be referred to as a sensory integration therapist. Like all other therapists your child will work with, this person is college educated. She will be involved in continuing education, and belong to one or more professional organizations.

Many daily living skills are difficult for children with autism to perform. An occupational therapist will work with a child to increase self-care skills and fine motor and gross motor skills, and to increase concentration and calming.

An OT will do a wide variety of things to increase your child's ability to function independently. If you need something to help your child compensate or adapt, ask the OT. If classroom equipment needs to be modified, the OT will most likely know how to do it. Problem solving is her specialty, and she can bring many solutions to situations that puzzle you.

LICENSED CLINICAL SOCIAL WORKERS

The licensed clinical social worker (LCSW) is no longer exclusively for families who have financial or social problems. The LCSW is a mental-health professional who deals with a variety of emotional and societal issues that bring about conflicts in life. LCSWs are college educated with a master's degree and are required to complete continuing education annually.

If a psychologist can be viewed as treating the mental health of an individual, the LCSW can be considered as the mental-health expert for society. He specializes in maintaining the social functioning of an individual in a group. The LCSW's goal is to create the best social situation possible for your child, whether it is in the family, a group home, or society in general.

Social workers can be helpful when an adult child is considered for placement in a group-home environment. An LCSW will also help a family determine whether they are getting the financial help they are entitled to and whether it is distributed properly, if that is a concern. They can help a family with many issues at the school and community levels, as well.

Emerging Treatment Programs

As you explore various options for your child's medical care, you will find many programs and treatment plans. Investigate and research all that are sound and reasonable. Your goal is to make your child the happiest, most well-adjusted person he can be. Be aware of programs that promise the impossible.

Many good treatment options are available. To learn more, consult with your child's physician or speak with other parents at your support group meeting. Don't try to reinvent the wheel; other people can provide you with a great deal of information. But remember that you must follow your own instincts and do what you think is best for your child and family.

Some controversial treatment options are out there. Some parents have reported that they felt taken advantage of in their attempt to find a cure for their child's autism. Even though there are websites and books proclaiming significant improvements with different treatments, not all of these have had their results tested under controlled conditions. Before deciding on alternative therapies, it is wise to discuss them with the person you know who is most knowledgeable about autism. You can use your mindfulness practice to slow down, relax, and breathe deeply before making any decisions.

NEURO-IMMUNE DYSFUNCTION SYNDROME (NIDS) PROTOCOL

Some research has suggested a link between autoimmune disorders, autism, and ADD. NIDS treatment protocol operates to balance the immune system in an effort to reduce the symptoms of autism. The results have been good according to some reports.

The treatment protocol involves looking for various markers including allergens, and viral and bacterial titers. For the patient's family, this means that blood and urine are analyzed for things that the child may be allergic to or that may indicate levels of exposure to certain viruses and bacterial infections. If unusual results are obtained, or allergies are determined, treatment can begin that is said to alleviate some of the symptoms of autism. Hyperbaric oxygen treatments (HOBT) are relatively new and some parents have been delighted with the results. HBOT is a medical treatment that enhances the body's natural healing process by inhalation of 100 percent oxygen in a total body chamber, where atmospheric pressure is increased and controlled.

Healing cannot take place without appropriate oxygen levels in the tissue. Most illnesses and injuries occur, and often linger, at the cellular or tissue level. In many cases, adequate oxygen cannot reach the damaged area and the body's natural healing ability is unable to function properly. Hyperbaric oxygen therapy provides this extra oxygen naturally and with minimal side effects.

Hyperbaric oxygen therapy can improve the quality of life of the patient in many areas when standard medicine is not working. Many conditions such as autism, stroke, cerebral palsy, head injuries, and chronic fatigue have responded favorably to HBOT.

However, any treatment such as this should be started only after careful research and discussion with your autism expert.

Some therapists use a technique called Greenspan or Floortime and also teach this method to parents. The theory is that getting down on the floor with a child will help develop better interaction and communication. Dr. Stanley Greenspan developed this technique, and the website to check is www .stanleygreenspan.com.

Try not to begin two or more therapies or diets simultaneously. If you have positive results, you will not be certain which treatment or diet was the effective one. Give a new therapy at least three months before you evaluate the results and then decide if you wish to continue.

Diet and Nutrition

There are diets that may help decrease some of the symptoms of autism, particularly a child's lack of focus and aggression. Some parents and professionals have seen success in two types of nutritional plans: the elimination of gluten and casein, the ketogenic diet, and the addition of B_6 vitamins. Following is a discussion of these three methods.

THE GFCF DIET

One of the most popular treatment plans involves the use of a gluten-free, casein-free (GFCF) diet. This means exactly what it says: A person on this diet ingests no glutens or caseins. It excludes all wheat, rye, barley, and oats from the diet as well as almost all milk products.

New research has emerged demonstrating success with specialized diets for autism. In a small Danish study in 2010 of children ages four to eleven, some children showed significant improvements after eight, twelve, and twenty-four months on a GFCF diet. Researchers at Penn State surveyed the parents of approximately 400 children with autism and found that a GFCF diet improved symptoms such as hyperactivity, tantrums, poor eye contact, and speech deficits, and physical ailments such as skin rashes and seizures for certain groups of children. Those who followed the diet closely and stayed on it for a minimum of six months showed the most improvement.

The idea of eliminating gluten and casein from the diet involves a theory that autism could potentially be a metabolic disorder or, as stated earlier, an autoimmune disease. The GFCF diet as a method of treatment is based on the premise that a child with autism is having a toxicological response to the molecule of gluten, and that the central nervous system (CNS) behavior is affected by the action of the molecule in a body that cannot tolerate it.

If you decide to begin this approach to treating autism, do your homework first. Many products have hidden gluten in them, and even one molecule can affect the success of the diet. Learn about gluten-free eating, as it would be a dramatic and difficult change for your family meals. Be aware that a large number of children who do not have autism have a problem with gluten. Your physician can help you determine whether the diet is right for your child and your family.

THE KETOGENIC DIET

A lesser-known dietary approach for ASD is the ketogenic diet. This diet has foods that have high fat, adequate protein, and are low in carbohydrates. This diet was originally developed to treat epilepsy.

The February 2003 study, "Application of a Ketogenic Diet in Children With Autistic Behavior: Pilot Study" published in the *Journal of Child Neurology* found that children on the diet presented with improvements in their social behavior and interactions, speech, cooperation, stereotype, and hyperactivity. All of this helped improve their learning. The children who could not stay on the diet were the most severely affected by autism; the ones who responded the best were affected mildly. The study reported that the children maintained the improvements from the diet even six months after the study was complete.

Again, before beginning any diet, please consult with your physician.

VITAMIN B$_6$

Vitamin B$_6$ is a very popular form of treatment. It is harmless if taken as directed, and the studies have shown positive results. Individuals require different levels of vitamin B$_6$, and if a person has a deficiency, the theory goes, taking large doses of the vitamin will assist him. If that is the case, autism could also be viewed as a vitamin deficiency, much like scurvy results from a lack of vitamin C. The key is balancing the B$_6$ intake with the other vitamins to utilize B$_6$ efficiently without causing a deficiency in another vitamin, which could in turn cause undesirable side effects. Magnesium is used to counteract the larger B$_6$ intake and has shown to be effective as well. It would be important to discuss any large intake of vitamins with your child's pediatrician.

Vitamin B$_6$ therapy has been thought by some to improve eye contact, reduce self-stimulating behaviors, reduce tantrums, improve social and environmental interactions, and improve speech. If you are interested in this therapy, contact the Autism Research Institute. Your physician may not know about the therapy, so the Institute could send some brochures.

Vitamin B$_6$ therapy is not a cure—the founders of the treatment will be the first to admit that. But with studies showing at least half of children responding favorably to megadoses of vitamins B$_6$ and normal supplements of vitamin B complex and magnesium, it is not something parents can easily disregard.

Important Points to Consider

Involvement in early intervention is critical to improve development and acquire skills in a child with autism.

- Important professionals in your child's life may be his physician, occupational therapist, physical therapist, speech therapist, and social worker.

- It is essential to work with professionals who feel right for you and your child. If you do not feel comfortable with them, continue looking until you find the best team.

- Try not to begin two or more therapies or diets simultaneously. If you have positive results, you will not be certain which treatment or diet was the effective one. Participate in a new therapy for at least three months before you evaluate the results and then decide if you wish to continue.

- There are alternative treatment options available that are known to help some children with autism, including a shift to a gluten-free, casein-free diet and treatment with B_6.

CHAPTER 17

Finding Support and Assistance

Many parents feel a sense of isolation when they learn their child has autism. Professionals can present the diagnosis in a way that feels very final and offers you little hope. You also may experience periods during your child's schooling in which you feel very alone if you are having challenges getting your child's needs met.

Though it is natural to want to isolate, this may not be the best thing for you or your child. Many forms of support are available to you so you do not feel so alone; you can find help while problem solving or determining what your child needs.

The Importance of Support

While independence is wonderful, too much of it can actually cause you to feel more isolated and alone. Have you ever considered that asking for help is not a sign of weakness, but actually a sign of courage and strength?

It requires vulnerability to ask for and receive support. Having the courage to face a problem requires us to feel safe enough to talk about the problem, identify solutions and alternatives, and develop a plan of action by talking with others, either friends or professionals.

There are five obstacles that can block you from receiving support.

1. *Believing that needing help is a sign of weakness.* Allowing yourself to be vulnerable is having the courage to ask for help, to admit that you are afraid, and to trust that someone will be there for you.

2. *Thinking you don't deserve help.* We all need help now and then. Handling everything by yourself is really hard. When you accept help, it can actually strengthen your relationships. Be selective when you ask for help. You'll want to share your feelings with someone who listens and cares, not someone who judges, criticizes, or blames you.

3. *Not speaking up to ask for help.* Sometimes you have people in your life who see what you need and offer to help before you ask. Most of the time you'll need to ask. The best way to ask is to be clear and direct, saying, "I'm having trouble with this. Can you help me, please?"

4. *Waiting for someone else to make the first move.* It's not always easy for other people to see when you need help. Maybe you put on a cheerful face or give off a vibe that you don't want to talk, so people don't know how to offer. Learning to ask for help can get your needs met.

5. *Giving up too easily.* It is wonderful when people respond immediately to our requests for help. However, sometimes we have to ask for help multiple times or from different people.

What Is Support?

Support allows you to receive help and experience relief through others who have "been there, done that." Support is learning to ask questions that you didn't even know existed. And support is one of the primary ways you will find peace in having a child with autism.

A lot of the reason parents have problems getting their own parents to understand how to handle their child with autism is simply difficulties knowing how to communicate or feeling unsure what to do. You may approach your own mother with your frustrations, but she has no frame of reference, not having had nor raised a child with autism herself. Your frustration may be received, whether you intend it that way or not, by her attempting to help. This may make you feel worse, because her suggestions may not work; she simply does not have the knowledge you may need.

IDENTIFYING THE BEST SUPPORT OPTIONS

This is the advantage of a support group. Those people know! They have been right where you are and you don't have to explain the entire autism spectrum to them in order to vent a little. Few things are more frustrating than needing to have a gripe session, but before you can launch into your frustration, having to give a twenty-minute speech to explain the issues that have caused your frustration to begin with.

If you need to find a physician or dentist, ask at your support group meeting. The people there will have suggestions and will be able to give you their opinion of the care their child received. Recommendations from people who may share concerns similar to yours are a great way to find the services your child needs.

A support group for families who have children with autism won't mind if you stagger into a meeting exhausted from a lack of sleep because your child only slept for thirty minutes the night before. They may have been up all night, too. They understand your need to find a babysitter who can handle autism for two hours so you can attend one of your other children's school conferences. They probably even have a list of names and phone numbers.

Above all, the members of a support group, just by their presence, will remind you that you aren't alone in your daily struggles. You will learn that they, too, worry about what will happen when their child is an adult—they have the same fears and concerns you have. They will reassure you that you did nothing to cause this to happen to your child and will rejoice with your victories and cry with your disappointments.

GIVING SUPPORT

As time goes by and autism and all its idiosyncrasies become second nature to you, you will find that you have a lot of knowledge and experience to impart to others. For some people it happens immediately and for others it takes a bit longer. You will go from being an observer to being a listener to being a parent who helps parents with newly diagnosed children. You will have ideas, solutions, and little tricks you have stumbled upon that will be of invaluable help to someone you may not even know yet.

One rule that should be followed in any support group is to not criticize other people for their decisions about treatment and therapy for autism. Remember to keep your comments and opinions positive and helpful. Treat all members with respect, even if you don't agree with them, because they are entitled to their opinions.

The most important thing you can remember about giving support is to withhold judgment. It is possible that you will meet someone who has different theories than yours on the causes and the best treatments for autism. These are unknowns right now, and it is more important to work together on coping than to spend valuable time and energy debating the issues. No one is totally right and no one is totally wrong. Autism support groups are full of parents trying to get by and do the best job they possibly can, and what they need is encouragement.

Much of dealing with autism is learning by trial and error. Participating in a support group allows you to learn from the experience of others; you will save a lot of frustration and irritation if you can avoid the mistakes others have made. When you have had some experience, then you can share what you have learned and help others as they begin their journey.

Finding the Right Support Group

Just as every treatment isn't right for your child, not every support group will be right for you. Some support groups are founded on a belief in a certain treatment. If you do not feel comfortable with the particular treatment that is the foundation for a support group, the group won't be a good fit for you. They provide specialized support for those who follow a certain theory, and that is fine, but don't ever join a group with the idea that you can change its focus. That isn't fair to them or you.

WHAT ARE THE DIFFERENCES?

There are many different kinds of support groups available. There are large ones and small ones, ones that meet weekly and ones that meet monthly, ones with and without babysitting provided, and ones that serve particular age groups. There is no single right way to have a support group. The goal is to create a community or family where the issues of raising a child with autism can be freely discussed.

If you have never been part of a support group, consider joining one that is general in its nature and approach. Their main emphasis should be on coping with autism and its behaviors, not to advocate a specific theory.

GENERAL DISABILITIES OR ASD SPECIFIC?

One of the first decisions to make in selecting the right support group for you is whether you want a group for parents of children with any disability or one that is only for parents of children with autism. There are good things about either type of group. Some of this may depend on the community in which you live—it may be hard to find a very specific support group if you live in a small town.

Groups that support families who have children with various disabilities bring a great deal of variety into a discussion and add to the group dynamics. If you have never been to a support meeting, you may think you would have little in common with a mother holding a baby that depends on a feeding tube. You will be surprised at how much you do have in common once you begin to talk and learn about each other's daily lives. Parents of hearing-impaired children will have a lot of advice about handling simple communication issues; even though their children may have receptive language, they know what a lack of expressive speech means to a family.

Walking into a support meeting for the very first time can be a little scary, but remember that everyone there was a newcomer once themselves. You'll want to find a meeting where you feel welcome.

One of the most significant benefits of a group that supports various disabilities is the way it will dispel your sense of isolation. When you see other parents dealing with issues far different from yours, yet just as disabling, and realize these parents are surviving, you will no longer feel as alone. Meeting people who deal with children who are physically and mentally challenged puts life into perspective and things become more manageable for all involved.

Groups that support only parents of children with autism also offer some great benefits. Parents who deal with autism on a daily basis are not going to so much as lift an eyebrow if your child empties out your purse and lines up its contents on the floor. They know what a meltdown is and won't stare at you when your child has one in the parking lot. They understand elopement and how frightening it is. And they won't assume your child will talk to them; they will understand the needs of a nonverbal child.

SPECIALIZED GROUPS

After some time, if you become involved in a particular treatment, you can even seek out a group that is devoted to discussion of that treatment. They will likely touch on general coping strategies as well, but the focus will center on a particular therapy. One advantage to a specialized support group is the information you can obtain from the experiences of the members. If you, for example, want to try a particular diet to treat your child's autism, it can be helpful to be around people who are using that eating plan. There is no reason to reinvent the wheel, so be there to learn and eventually share with others.

All types of support groups have strong points that should be considered. It is likely that a group for general disabilities will include some families who have children with autism. You may be limited in your choices because of location or scheduling issues, but keep looking until you find one that works for you. Making it a point to join and regularly attend a support group is one step you can take that will help your life immensely.

Forming a Support Group

If you have discovered that there is no support group in your local area, you might consider starting one of your own. You have the qualifications as the parent of a child on the autism spectrum. Beginning a support group is easy and takes a minimum of time and money.

Begin by talking with your child's physician. She might want to get involved on some level, and at the very least will tell other patients about the group. You can also mention your group at your child's special-education department, and if you live near a community mental health center, connecting with them would be helpful, too.

ORGANIZING

After you have some experts aware of your support group's "birth," begin to organize by setting preliminary schedules and goals. Meeting once a week is standard practice; you can also have special functions when the group is established, but for now start with weekly meetings. Compare your schedule to other schedules in your community to look for potential conflicts; for example, if every religious center in town has a Wednesday night service, choose another evening.

Churches or other religious centers could be a good place for support group meetings. If you are a member of a church, synagogue, or mosque, ask if they would be willing to donate a room for a meeting. Have members bring soft drinks, water, cookies, and muffins and you will be all ready to go.

Your next step is to find a space that would work for your meeting. Your local library may have a room they will let you use at no charge. Senior centers and community meeting halls are also possibilities. Your home is an option but it should be your last choice; you don't want the stress of making your home "just-so" when you want to create a supportive environment for families. Make fliers and posters to let people know where and when you will be meeting.

The next step is easy. Put out cookies, coffee, and tea, and wait for people. They will show up if you have the word out. Spend time getting to know people and let your group evolve naturally. You can have guest speakers if you want and think it would be helpful. Many large support groups have started from small beginnings such as this. You may be creating a new family!

ACTIVITIES FOR SUPPORT GROUPS

Many groups have planned activities. They may be educational or just for fun. They can be to raise money to help the support group in different ways or to funnel toward an autism awareness fund that the group would like to support. Whatever your goals, plan ahead to get as much out of the activity as possible.

Guest speakers should be scheduled about three months or more before you would like them to speak. That will allow you to organize discussions that work up to the speaker's topic and create greater interest. When you contact someone about speaking to your group, ask about fees and what topic they would like to discuss. If fees are involved you may be able to cover them with a fund you have for this purpose. If there is a speaker you really want to bring in but the fee is higher than your budget, plan a fundraiser to cover the expenses.

Annual activities, such as a holiday party or a summer picnic, are common in groups that meet regularly. A yearly calendar can help your group stay organized, especially when an annual event requires a lot of advance planning. Picnics often require that an area of a park be reserved, and holiday parties will need a comfortable space for adults and children of all ages. Again, you may want to establish a fund to cover such activities.

Another activity that your group might take advantage of is attending a national autism seminar. Throughout the year, many such seminars are held for two to four days. If two or three of your group attend and bring back notes and information they could share with the rest of the group, it could be helpful for everyone. Groups will sometimes plan for one seminar yearly and coordinate a fundraising event to cover the expenses.

A great way to generate funds for your support group is to have all the families get together for a combined garage sale. If everyone donates to the sale and helps with advertising and set-up, your group could make a substantial amount of money that could be used for various activities.

Support on the Internet

The Internet may be one of the greatest inventions of the twentieth century. Never before in human history have so many people been instantly in contact in any part of the world at any time of the day or night. If you don't have a computer, your public library will have several you can use for short periods of time.

ONLINE AUTISM COMMUNITIES

An autism community on the Internet is much like any other community. It has information, people, discussions, planned meetings, chat rooms, shopping, and many personal opinions from the community population, as well as medical professionals. You can find resources that can be trusted; just remember to pay attention to the source of the information.

One of the major advantages to autism communities on the Internet is the accessibility factor. They are literally open twenty-four hours a day, seven days a week. They are good for middle-of-the-night ranting and raving, and they are wonderful for people who live in isolated areas. If you have a work schedule that prohibits your attending a real-life support group, the Internet is your next best bet. And if you have a real-life support group, the knowledge you gain on the Internet can enhance your group meetings.

Appendix B at the end of this book has sources on the Internet that are valuable for anyone close to a child with autism. If you are new to the world of cyberspace, find a good book to help you get around on the web and find the resources you are searching for. Check out various communities and discover the volume of information that can help you as you learn about autism.

OTHER ONLINE COMMUNITIES

There are many communities on the Internet that you will find useful. Don't limit yourself to sites just related to autism. There are many other resources to help you take care of yourself and meet your own needs, and your children will benefit from it.

Communities for spirituality can be helpful for people who feel that the spiritual part of their lives must be functional for their lives to be complete. There are many sites for every known faith that are managed by people who believe as you do. Joining such a community will enrich your own life and, by extension, the lives of your children.

If you are a news junkie, the Internet is the place to be. All of the major news services can be found online as well as thousands of reliable news sources that may be brand new to you. Sometimes parents become so involved with a child's disability, they forget to stay in touch with the rest of the world. On the Internet, you can do that at your convenience, not on a television network's schedule.

If you have a need or are just looking for something for fun, if it is for business or entertainment, or if you are looking for something for yourself or for your children, you will be able to find a community for it online. Use search engines to find what you are looking for and just see where it might take you.

MAILING LISTS AND NEWSLETTERS

One primary method for communication used online by support groups is a mailing list. This is like a discussion that is spread out over a period of time. People subscribe to a mailing list and e-mails are generated from one person to the entire group. Any number of people can answer a given e-mail, and their response goes out to all members of the list. It is much like standing in the middle of a party and carrying on several conversations at once. People on mailing lists tend to become friends and sometimes even expand their friendships off the list, sometimes meeting in real life.

Newsletters are another source of information for parents of children with special needs. Websites will often have a weekly, biweekly, or monthly newsletter that is e-mailed to subscribers at no charge. The benefit of these newsletters is that someone else is doing the research for you. All you have to do is visit the site where they have the information posted. This can be a great service but be sure that any newsletters you receive are sent by sources you can trust.

Important Points to Consider

In modern culture, independence is important. However, when you become independent to the point of being defensive, it can lead to feelings of isolation.

- Asking for help is a sign of strength and will make your life a whole lot easier than struggling to do things on your own all the time.

- Finding the right support group can make a huge difference in how you can effectively cope with the daily challenges of raising a child with autism.

O One of the most significant benefits of a support group is that it can dispel your sense of isolation and let you know you are not alone.

O Use discernment when you are considering new treatment options and online environments.

Appendix A: Glossary

Activities of daily living (ADL)
The activities that each person engages in daily for personal care and hygiene. Dressing and bathing are examples.

American Sign Language (ASL)
The primary sign language used in the United States. It was developed for people with deafness and is often conceptually based.

Applied behavior analysis (ABA)
A therapy method that uses positive reinforcement to encourage appropriate behaviors that will help an individual with autism function in society. One approach to ABA is the Lovaas method, after Dr. Ivar Lovaas.

Attention deficit disorder (ADD)
A developmental disorder that is characterized by a short attention span and a lack of concentration on tasks.

Attention deficit hyperactivity disorder (ADHD)
A developmental disorder that is composed of ADD and hyperactivity in the same individual.

Auditory processing disorder (APD)
A disorder in which language is heard correctly but not understood or not processed correctly by the brain.

Augmentative and alternative communication (AAC)
A communication aid to assist people with limited or no verbal ability. A communication board is the most commonly used tool.

Autism
A neurological disorder characterized by communication difficulties, sensory problems, and socialization issues. Usually appears between eighteen and twenty-four months.

Autism Society of America (ASA)
One of the leading autism organizations in the United States.

Autism spectrum disorder (ASD)
A collection of disabilities characterized by symptoms such as impaired verbal ability and social dysfunction.

Beneficiary
The recipient of a trust fund, life insurance policy, or other assets and funds that have been designated to go to that person.

Diagnostic and Statistical Manual of Mental Disorders
A publication used to diagnose autism spectrum and other disorders. The fifth edition (DSM-5) is the most current version.

Echolalia
The verbal repetition of words without using those words for any communication or meaning.

Elopement
The tendency of a child with autism to "escape" her environment and wander off, usually with no particular direction in mind.

Expressive speech
The ability to utilize spoken language to convey ideas, thoughts, and feelings.

Facilitated communication
A method of communication that uses the aid of another person for physical and emotional support.

Flapping
The movement of the hand and forearm by a child or adult with autism that mimics a wave but occurs due to overstimulation, either physical or emotional.

Free appropriate public education (FAPE)
Programs for education that meet a student's needs with the provision of adequate support.

Gluten-free, casein-free (GFCF) diet
A diet used by many parents of children on the autism spectrum. The diet excludes all gluten and casein products.

High-functioning autism (HFA)
A form of autism that is much less disabling, as an individual has verbal ability and varying degrees of social understanding. IQ will be measured at eighty or above.

Imaginative play
The ability to play with objects using imagination. For example, toy cars, people, and houses can be a town in which an entire scenario is played out.

Inclusive education
A term used interchangeably with mainstreaming. Refers to a child with special needs having access to the same classroom as if he were not a child with special needs.

Individualized Education Program (IEP)
An official plan, written on a yearly basis, that is developed at a meeting with parents, teachers, therapists, and other experts involved in the education of a child with special needs.

Individuals with Disabilities Education Act (IDEA)
A United States congressional act that dictates all the rights children with disabilities have to receive full educational benefits from public schools.

IQ (intelligence quotient)
The number that is considered a standard for measuring a person's intelligence and capacity for understanding.

Least restrictive environment (LRE)
An educational term referring to the classroom or environment a student attends daily that provides the least amount of restriction to ensure safety and the most social and educational interaction.

Licensed clinical social worker (LCSW)

A mental-health professional licensed by a state to help individuals and families.

Low-functioning autism (LFA)

A more severe form of autism with IQ measuring at below seventy.

Meltdown

The total loss of behavioral control by a person with autism due to sensory overload.

Neuro-immune dysfunction syndrome (NIDS)

The possible connection between neuro-immune and/or autoimmune dysfunction and conditions such as autism, ADD, Alzheimer's, ALS, CFS/CFIDS, MS, and other immune-mediated diseases.

Obsessive-compulsive disorder (OCD)

A disorder in which a person is obsessed with unwanted thoughts and feels the need to act out compulsive behaviors.

Occupational therapist or occupational therapy (OT)

A therapist who works with a patient to improve fine motor skills as well as developing solutions for practical day-to-day living as deficits are accommodated.

Parallel play

Playing beside another child, but playing independently and not interacting with that child.

Physical therapist or physical therapy (PT)

A therapist or therapy that works to increase the functionality of gross motor skills.

Picture Exchange Communication System (PECS)

A communication tool that uses photographs and/or drawings to replace words for language.

Receptive language

Hearing spoken language from another person and deciphering it into a meaningful mental picture or thought pattern, which is understood and then used by the recipient.

Rett Syndrome (RS)

Rett Syndrome is a genetic neurological disorder seen almost exclusively in females and found in a variety of racial and ethnic groups worldwide. It is characterized by normal or near normal development until six to eighteen months of life. A period of temporary stagnation or regression follows, during which the child loses communication skills and purposeful use of the hands.

Selective serotonin reuptake inhibitors (SSRIs)

A group of medications used for depression, anxiety, and the control of obsessive-compulsive behaviors, including Prozac, Zoloft, Paxil, and Luvox.

Sensory overload

The reaction a child with autism has when more senses are being stimulated than she has the ability to process.

Service animal

An animal that is trained to work with and meet the needs of a person with special needs.

Tic

A brief, repetitive, purposeless, non-rhythmic, involuntary movement or sound. Tics that produce movement are called "motor tics," while tics that produce sound are called "vocal tics" or "phonic tics." Tics tend to occur in bursts or "bouts."

Tourette Syndrome (TS)

Also known as Tourette's Syndrome or Tourette's disorder, this is a fairly common childhood-onset condition that may be associated with features of many other conditions. This syndrome is characterized by "tics."

Treatment and Education of Autistic and Related Communication-Handicapped Children (TEACCH)

A method of teaching children with communication deficits that encourages communication with picture boards or other assistive devices.

Appendix B:
Additional Resources

The American Academy of Child and Adolescent Psychiatry

3615 Wisconsin Ave. NW
Washington, DC 20016-3007
202-966-7300
www.aacap.org
The American Academy of Child and Adolescent Psychiatry provides important information as a public service to assist parents and families in their most important roles.

Autism Research Institute

4182 Adams Avenue
San Diego, CA 92116
866-366-3361
www.autism.com
The Autism Research Institute (ARI), a nonprofit organization, was established in 1967. ARI is primarily devoted to conducting research, and to disseminating the results of research, on the causes of autism and on methods of preventing, diagnosing, and treating autism and other severe behavioral disorders of childhood. They provide information based on research to parents and professionals throughout the world.

Autism Society

4340 East-West Highway, Suite 350
Bethesda, MD 20814
301-657-0881 or 1-800-3AUTISM
www.autism-society.org
ASA has over 200 chapters covering nearly every state, reaching out to individuals with autism and their families with information, support, and encouragement.

Autism Speaks

NEW YORK
1 East 33rd Street, 4th Floor
New York, NY 10016
212-252-8584

PRINCETON
1060 State Road, 2nd Floor
Princeton, NJ 08540
609-228-7310

LOS ANGELES
6330 San Vicente Blvd., Suite 401
Los Angeles, CA 90048
323-549-0500

Field Offices

ATLANTA
900 Circle 75 Parkway, Suite 445
Atlanta, GA 30339
(770) 451-0570

BOSTON
85 Devonshire Street, 9th Floor
Boston, MA 02109
(617) 726-1515

CENTRAL FLORIDA/ORLANDO
557 N. Wymore Road, Bldg. A, Suite 101
Maitland, FL 32751
(407) 478-6330

CHARLOTTE
8604 Cliff Cameron Drive, Suite 144
Charlotte, NC 28269

CHICAGO
Regency Office Plaza, Suite 304
2700 River Road
Des Plaines, IL 60018
(224) 567-8573

CINCINNATI
(513) 504-3999

CLEVELAND
4700 Rockside Rd, Suite 420
Independence, OH 44131
(216) 524-2842

COLUMBUS
470 Glenmont Avenue
Columbus, OH 43214
(614) 563-6320

DALLAS
6380 LBJ Freeway, Suite 285
Dallas, TX 75240
(972) 960-6227

GREATER DELAWARE VALLEY
216 Haddon Avenue, Suite 403
Westmont, NJ 08108
(856) 858-5400

LEXINGTON SOUTH CAROLINA
863 Corley Mill Road
Lexington, SC 29072
(803) 520-8080

LONG ISLAND
382 Main Street, 1st floor
Port Washington, NY 11050
(631) 521-7853

MIAMI
5805 Blue Lagoon Drive, Suite 170
Miami, FL 33126
(786) 235-1165

PHOENIX
668 N. 44th Street, Suite 300
Phoenix, AZ 85008
(602) 685-1161

PITTSBURGH
8035 McKnight Road, Suite 302
Pittsburgh, PA 15237
(412) 367-4571

SEATTLE
159 Western Avenue West, Suite 454A
Seattle, WA 98119
(206) 464-5182

ST. LOUIS
1121 Olivette Executive Pkwy., Suite 220
St. Louis, MO 63132
(314) 989-1003

WASHINGTON, D.C.
1990 K Street, NW, Second Floor
Washington, DC 20006
(202) 955-3111

WEST PALM BEACH
1475 Centrepark Blvd., Suite 115
West Palm Beach, FL 33401
(561) 465-0050

www.autismspeaks.org

Autism Speaks is the largest autism science and advocacy organization in the United States. It funds research into the causes, prevention, treatments, and a cure for autism. It also increases awareness of autism spectrum disorders, and advocates for the needs of individuals with autism and their families.

The BHARE Foundation

523 Newberry
Elk Grove, IL 60007
847-352-7678

http://bhare.org

The Brenen Hornstein Autism Research & Education (BHARE) Foundation's top priority is to fund research that will lead to a cure for autism. Good summaries for parents are available along with information regarding project funding.

Children's Rights Council

1296 Cronson Blvd., Suite 3086
Crofton, MD 21114
301-459-1220

www.crckids.org

The Children's Rights Council (CRC) is a national nonprofit organization based near Washington, DC, that works to assure children meaningful and continuing contact with both their parents and extended family regardless of the parents' marital status.

Doug Flutie Jr. Foundation for Autism

P.O. Box 767
Framingham, MA 01701
508-270-8855 or 1-866-3AUTISM

www.flutiefoundation.org
www.facebook.com/flutiefoundation

The Doug Flutie Jr. Foundation for Autism supports families affected by autism spectrum disorder, and promotes awareness for the disorder. They fund organizations that provide direct services, grants, education, advocacy, and recreational opportunities for individuals with autism and their families.

Families for Early Autism Treatment (FEAT)

P.O. Box 255722
Sacramento, CA 95865-5722

www.feat.org

Families for Early Autism Treatment (FEAT) is a California-based organization with chapters in several states. Among other things, FEAT publishes one of the most comprehensive, informative, and activist newsletters in the autism community.

Federation of State Medical Boards of the United States, Inc.

400 Fuller Wiser Road
Euless, TX 76039
817-868-4000

www.fsmb.org

The Federation of State Medical Boards (FSMB) website allows you to research any serious disciplinary actions or professional peer reviews against a physician you are considering for your child.

From Emotions to Advocacy (FETA)
www.fetaweb.com

Wrightslaw: From Emotions to Advocacy: The Special Education Survival Guide, Second Edition by Pam and Pete Wright, is an excellent resource for special education information. Fetaweb.com is the companion website to WrightsLaw.com.

International Society for Augmentative and Alternative Communication (ISAAC)

312 Dolomite Drive, Suite 216
Toronto, ON M3J 2N2, Canada
1-905-850-6848
www.isaac-online.org
The International Society for Augmentative and Alternative Communication (ISAAC) is an organization devoted to advancing the field of augmentative and alternative communication (AAC). The Mission of ISAAC is to promote the best possible communication for people with complex communication needs.

My Autism Team

www.myautismteam.com
My Autism Team is a free, supportive social network for parents of kids with autism.

The National Autistic Society

393 City Road
London, EC1V 1NG, United Kingdom
44 (0)20 7833 2299
www.autism.org.uk
The National Autistic Society (NAS) is the UK's foremost organization for people with autism and those who care for them, spearheading national and international initiatives and providing a strong voice for autism. The NAS works in many areas to help people with autism live their lives with as much independence as possible.

National Organization of Social Security Claimants' Representatives (NOSSCR)

560 Sylvan Ave., Suite 2200
Englewood Cliffs, NJ 07632
201-567-4228
www.nosscr.org
The National Organization of Social Security Claimants' Representatives (NOSSCR) has a referral service for claimants looking for a private attorney and Social Security benefit information and representation. They also have a caller hotline number for SSI children's benefits. The referral is free; the attorney will charge for the representation if the claim is successful.

No Child Left Behind

U.S. Department of Education
400 Maryland Ave. SW
Washington, DC 20202
800-872-5327 (800-USA-LEARN)
http://ed.gov/nclb
The No Child Left Behind website includes a simple overview of the legislation, key dates to remember, frequently asked questions, information about what is happening in states across the country, and more importantly, where you can go to learn more and become involved. The goal of No Child Left Behind is to create the best educational opportunities for our nation's children and to ensure that they have every opportunity to succeed. The new revised legislation should make it much more effective.

Patient-Centered Guides Autism Center
www.oreilly.com/medical/autism/
The Patient-Centered Guides Autism Center is for families of those living with a pervasive developmental disorder. Much of the material here is for those in the middle of the autistic spectrum, particularly those with a diagnosis of PDD-NOS or Atypical PDD or those still trying to find a correct diagnosis. You can find articles and resources about PDDs, diagnosis, drug treatments, therapies, supplements, education, insurance, family life, other coping topics, and resources.

Social Security Administration
800-772-1213
www.ssa.gov
This is the website where you can apply for disability benefits for your child, get your supplemental security statements, and apply for appeals.

WrightsLaw.com
www.wrightslaw.com
WrightsLaw.com is one of the most thorough websites regarding autism and special education. Parents, advocates, educators, and attorneys come to WrightsLaw.com for accurate, up-to-date information about special-education law and advocacy for children with disabilities.

The Nonverbal System
If you enjoyed this book, you'll also love the Nonverbal System. Now, you can learn the same system Marci Lebowitz has used to teach more than 1,000 families how to effortlessly communicate with their nonverbal child with autism. The program guides parents and professionals on how to deeply understand, relate with, and calm children with autism.
www.thenonverbalsystem.com

Praise for the Nonverbal System
"Marci's Nonverbal System is absolutely wonderful. I'd recommend it to any parent who is searching for how to deeply relate with, understand, and communicate with their nonverbal child with autism. You'll be so glad you did."—Patricia Genevose (parent of nonverbal twelve-year-old)

"I've tried everything else and none of it has worked. Marci's system is so different and boy does it work!"—Danelle Shouse (parent of nonverbal five-year-old)

Appendix C:
Frequently Asked Questions about Autism

What causes autism?

At this time, we do not know of a singular cause of autism. Scientists have identified what may be a number of genetic, non-genetic, and environmental factors that could contribute to a child developing autism.

Environmental risk factors that have been identified can occur before and during birth. They include advanced parental age at time of conception (either mother or father), maternal illness during pregnancy, extreme prematurity and very low birth weight, and certain difficulties during birth, particularly those involving periods of oxygen deprivation to the baby's brain. Mothers exposed to high levels of pesticides and air pollution may also be at higher risk of having a child with autism.

It is important to keep in mind that these factors, by themselves, do not cause autism. Rather, in combination with genetic risk factors, they may increase risk.

Who develops autism spectrum disorder (ASD)?

Autism is usually evident by the age of three, though diagnosis may be made as early as twelve to eighteen months, and as late as four to six years (sometimes even later). According to the Center for Disease Control, about one in sixty-eight children are diagnosed with ASD. Autism affects people of all racial, ethnic, and socioeconomic groups.

What does it mean to be "on the spectrum"?

Each individual with autism is unique. Some on the autism spectrum have exceptional abilities visually, in music, and academics. About 40 percent have intellectual disability (IQ less than 70), and many have normal to above-average intelligence. Many persons on the spectrum take deserved pride in their distinctive abilities and unique ways of viewing the world. Others with autism have significant disability and are unable to live independently. About 25 percent of individuals with ASD are nonverbal but learn to communicate using other means. Some children will need ongoing supervision, while others, with the right support, may pursue higher education and fulfilling jobs.

Index